"Many people assume that becoming a 'do gooder' requires changing who they are—to become like Mother Teresa or Gandhi. But Jonathan Golden knows better. He argues that embracing who God made you to be actually helps you contribute to the common good. Jonathan has found a way to make a difference to thousands of people in Rwanda and in the United States. Read his book and you'll learn how to do the same."

—**Gabe Lyons**, founder of Q and author of *The Next Christians*

"Calling and courage—Jonathan Golden leads by example on these leadership attributes. I've had the privilege of trekking with him and Land of A Thousand Hills Coffee for the last seven years. He has found his calling, and as you read his story, you'll understand why he's a good fit to guide you as you discover your own!"

—**Brad Lomenick**, author of *The Catalyst Leader*

"Jonathan Golden is one of the few voices I listen to on the topics of calling and purpose. He has proven his approach works in both his personal and professional lives. *Be You. Do Good.* is a practical and powerful book to help you find a life of meaning. Finally, a tool to help people find freedom to live as God made them to be!"

—**Jonathan Merritt**, author of *Jesus Is Better Than You Imagined* and senior columnist for Religion News Service

"*Be You. Do Good.* is a tremendous resource as you are seeking your life's calling. Whether you are a social entrepreneur or in career transition, this book will provide real-life examples of how to hone in on your mission, be generous, and influence people. Read it and get started doing good!"

—**Dale Partridge**, bestselling author
and founder of StartupCamp.com

"I remember so well the first time I met Jonathan and began learning about the incredible work and mission of Land of a Thousand Hills Coffee. I had never really heard of a direct trade business model, where each person in the supply chain, from the farmers to the salespeople, were considered equally integral and valuable to the company. It gave me hope that doing good business and treating everyone involved with respect and dignity do not have to be mutually exclusive. Rwanda has been through so much, and to see Jonathan engage the work of redemption in such a place gives me hope that we all can take part in the process, even just by sipping coffee! Read this book and you too will find out how you can *do good*!"

—**David Carr**, drummer of the band Third Day

"Wondering what God has for you? Jonathan Golden has been helping people discover and pursue their unique callings for over a decade, and I'm confident he can help you find yours. He and his team at Land of a Thousand Hills Coffee have made a lasting impression on my home nation of Rwanda, helping our people find their work. His story and ours is one of redemption. Yours can be too as you read this book!"

—**Edouard Bamporiki**, member of parliament
and Commissioner of Human Rights, Unity and
the Fight Against the Genocide, Rwanda

"The title itself captures the core essence of Jonathan's personal biography and journey: *Be You. Do Good.* Pursue what makes you come alive. Jonathan gives us not just inspiration and theory but rather a personal testimony of how the truths of God's unique design and calling in our lives plays out in the stories of his people. Jonathan does a masterful job of revealing practical truths through the story of his own journey of discovery and impact."

—**Todd Wilson**, founder of Exponential
and author of *More: Find Your Personal Calling
and Live Life to the Fullest Measure*

"Jonathan is the real deal. When it comes to saying yes to God's call without knowing what lies ahead, Jonathan writes with authority. Because he's said the brave yes to God's call, countless lives have been changed, including ours. We look forward to being part of the Rwandan story as we launch our own Land of a Thousand Hills Coffeehouse in Cypress Springs, Texas."

—**Melinda and Gary Bodukoglu**, entrepreneurs

"Being in a band mirrors almost every one of the twelve journeys, from 'Be who you are' to 'Pursue what makes you come alive.' The one that resonated the most with me was 'Growing little by little.' . . . In the moment it may feel frustrating to grow so gradually—one step here, one small step there—but I can promise you that in retrospect you will understand and actually savor the fact that you worked hard for what you earned. . . . Jonathan Golden will help you learn to stop throwing your hands in the air and yelling at the sky, '*Why, God?* Why aren't things happening now?' and start asking, '*What*, God? What can I learn in this season of waiting on what's next?'"

—**Steven Christian**, member of the band Anberlin

**BE YOU.
DO GOOD.**

BE YOU.
DO GOOD.

HAVING THE GUTS TO PURSUE
WHAT MAKES YOU
COME ALIVE

JONATHAN DAVID GOLDEN

BakerBooks
a division of Baker Publishing Group
Grand Rapids, Michigan

Published by Baker Books
a division of Baker Publishing Group
P.O. Box 6287, Grand Rapids, MI 49516-6287
www.bakerbooks.com

Printed in the United States of America

Library of Congress Cataloging-in-Publication Data
Golden, Jonathan David, 1966–
    Be you. Do good : having the guts to pursue what makes you come alive / Jonathan David Golden.
        pages cm
    Includes bibliographical references.
    ISBN 978-0-8010-1877-0 (pbk.)
    1. Vocation—Christianity. I. Title.
BV4740.G64 2016
248.4—dc23   2015034259

The author is represented by ChristopherFerebee.com, attorney and literary agent.

Some names and details have been changed to protect the privacy of the individuals involved.

16   17   18   19   20   21   22   7   6   5   4   3   2   1

Contents

Contents

Foreword

A lot of us want to live a life of meaning and passion.

We want our lives to count for something more than simply going to work and paying the mortgage (though I do recommend doing both). Many of us want to impact others and make a difference in the world today. We've deemed, at some point in our lives, that what we do with our days should *matter*. In a phrase, you might say you want to *Be You. Do Good.*

But if we're really honest, some of us aren't holding our breath in anticipation anymore.

For starters, we're not really expecting God to do something *right now*.

We know that back in "the Bible days," God called Abraham to "get up and go," Moses to lead his people to freedom, Esther to save a whole nation, and the disciples to share his message of grace. We can see how God used people like St. Patrick to share the Good News in Ireland and Dietrich Bonhoeffer to make a courageous stand. But today? We're not really expecting that God has anything spectacular up his divine sleeve right *now*.

Not this week. And we're not really expecting God's whimsical engagement with the world to happen right *here*.

We'll concede that spiritual rock stars like Mother Teresa in Calcutta, Katie Davis in Uganda, Archbishop Bishop Desmond Tutu in South Africa, and Shane Claiborne in Philadelphia have been specially tapped by God to do his will *someplace else*. After all, we reason, if God's really about doing something important, the chances are slim that the epicenter would be right where we're standing. What are the odds? It seems too unlikely.

So if we've bought the lie that God's not up to something right *now*, and not right *here*, then the logical extension is that God probably wouldn't use someone like *us*.

But what if God *is* engaging the world here and now? And what if God does want to use someone exactly like you?

In fact, what if God could *only* use someone exactly like you?

You see where this is heading. I think you can make a difference in this world. You can be you and do good!

When I first met Jonathan Golden, I shared with my wife that I'd met an amazing guy who is a social entrepreneur, Anglican priest, and MacGyver all rolled into one. Jonathan's canny knack for getting things done—things that don't quite seem possible to everyone else—has been a blessing to God's kingdom and to the world. But Jonathan's not content to simply do "his" thing with God in the world. No, Jonathan wants to equip others to find and embrace their unique God-given callings.

Very specifically, he wants *you* to find *yours*.

Jonathan and I agree: not only is God up to something *here* and something *now*, but God's instrument of choice happens to be *you*. If you're feeling flattered, you should be. As unlikely as it seems, God has chosen you and me to be divine agents in the world today. When you own that, everything changes.

Wait, wait, Bob, you may protest. *I'm super ordinary.*

Great. So is Jonathan. Me too. As unlikely as it seems, radically ordinary people just happen to be God's secret agents here on earth. (Any of those spiritual rock stars worth their salt will confirm this.)

Sure, Bob, you still protest, *but isn't it like solving a Rubik's Cube to figure out what God wants me to do?*

Some people think so. But I don't. And Jonathan doesn't.

In fact, Jonathan has spent years coaching and inspiring ordinary people like you—young and old, extroverts and introverts, students and employees, accountants and engineers, artists and musicians—to pursue what makes them come alive. He believes not only that God created you uniquely, for a purpose, but also that discovering that purpose is not at all complicated. It's actually *really* doable.

Friend, you've been made to live a life that's fully engaged by being exactly who God made you to be.

Right here.

Right now.

You were created to make a difference—to *Be You. Do Good.*

Bob Goff
Chief Balloon Inflater
Author of *Love Does*

Introduction

Let's Find Your True Calling

Is something gnawing deep inside of you to make a difference in this world? Are you longing to feel that God created you for and with a purpose? Does the whole idea of calling sound inviting but also confusing?

If so, you are like a lot of people I've had the privilege of working with through the years.

In my experience as a life coach, pastor, and social entrepreneur, I've enjoyed the cool gift of listening to folks and leading them as they consider their life callings. Your calling, or life's work, is what gives you purpose. It is what makes you unique and is your gift to the world. *That means that you are a gift to the world*. As you start using that gift, you will flourish and experience greater peace. Those around you will too.

Over many cups of coffee on the front porch of my office, exploring the variety of ways people I've met have been called, I've found a few things:

God calls us to himself.

Yes, he wants to hang out with you to be in relationship with you.

God calls us to be ourselves.

He doesn't want you to be someone else. He wants you to be who he has created you to be. Yes, flaws and all.

God calls us to do good.

He wants us to actually do something to make a difference in the world he loves.

He wants you to be you, and to do good. It really is that simple. God wants to have a vibrant relationship with you, God wants you to discover who he created you to be, and God wants you to partner with him to accomplish good in the world.

In the pages that follow, we'll explore together twelve adventures that will help you find your calling:

1. *Let go of the myths.* We have to start by clearing the air.
2. *Be who you are.* The first step in living your calling is to simply be your authentic self. Be you.
3. *Use what you have.* If it's your calling, you have what you need and can start today.
4. *Get what you can.* Reach out to others to get more of the resources you'll need.
5. *Follow the inkling.* Don't wait. Follow the inkling by taking a first step.

6. *Pursue what makes you come alive.* Notice and embrace the kind of work that makes you come alive.

7. *Find a people to serve.* It's not all about you. Notice and move toward the people you've been called to serve. Do good.

8. *Grow little by little.* Don't expect immediate seismic shifts. Plan to keep growing and developing.

9. *March through challenges.* Expect obstacles and soldier through them.

10. *Follow but don't force.* Remember that there is a *Caller*! Follow God's leading, but don't force.

11. *Stand back up.* When your calling stalls and you feel defeated, stand back up and keep going.

12. *Stay open to new possibilities.* Though it's tempting to hope that our callings are discoverable and then stay the same, God continues to call us into fresh expressions of who we were made to be.

Today the company I founded, Land of a Thousand Hills, is a multimillion-dollar coffee venture that is doing cutting-edge community development in Rwanda while providing excellent specialty coffee to churches, coffee shops, and grocery stores in America. We are now franchising and creating coffee-drinking communities across the United States. Maybe you've already tasted a good cup of coffee from Rwanda. But the road has not been easy, safe, certain, or straight.

I invested my own money to launch the venture. I had years when I didn't know if we were going to make it. My family has had to navigate a lot of pressures we would have avoided had I decided only to pastor my church, keep my consulting business, and ignore the inkling I felt God was giving me. Along the way I've kept track of the adventure. This book is the result, and I'm confident it can help you.

For over ten years now I've been working with the Rwandan people to do good, and I'm amazed at what God has accomplished. Every time I sit on one of those Rwandan hills and listen to the sounds of hope, my faith is rekindled and I'm filled with joy.

I've discovered my calling.

Let's go find yours.

– 1 –

In the Valley of Bukonya

Let Go of the Myths

"God spends the day elsewhere, but he sleeps in Rwanda."

This is a saying among those who live in the East African nation most famous for a mass genocide in the 1990s, and it draws on the belief that the Almighty hasn't forgotten the people of Rwanda. God may attend to other matters, they say, but he always comes back here.

Each time I visit, I know exactly what they mean.

Rwanda is the kind of place you go when you doubt God's existence and need to rekindle your faith. Warm sunlight bathes the lush, green landscape. People who once slaughtered each other by the hundreds work side by side while giggling children in worn but well-kept clothing play. At times, I'll be driving through a village and sense the Holy Spirit running alongside my truck with a smile on his face.

The valley of Bukonya is one of the most transcendent places in Rwanda. Though much changes in my life year to year—gains and losses, challenges and successes—this valley remains the same: beautiful green hills and exuberant people. The coffee company I founded, Land of a Thousand Hills, has a washing station there.

If you've never seen coffee processed, it is quite a sight to behold. After picking coffee cherries in the early morning, farmers walk, run, or ride their bikes, sometimes for eight hours, in order to deliver the work of their hands to the Land of a Thousand Hills coffee washing station. The cherries are weighed on an old-fashioned scale, and farmers receive their day's pay, often four times as much as they were paid before partnering with Land of a Thousand Hills. The coffee cherries are then placed in a flotation tank. The bad cherries float because insects have burrowed into them and trapped air inside. The good ones sink, are released through a door at the bottom of the tank, and flow into a chute. The chute delivers the cherries to our custom-made de-pulping machine. The machine has five textured discs that spin rapidly, removing the pulp and leaving the coffee beans. Coffee cherries go in, and the coffee beans come out.

The beans are then automatically sorted by the machine according to size. A series of screens allow the different-sized beans to drop into various channels which, like small rivers, direct the beans to the washing tanks. Once washed, the beans go into the fermentation tanks, where they stay for eight to twelve hours. This removes the sugary mucilage layer that stops the fermentation process and is what ensures a good cup of coffee. After that, the coffee, which is now known as parchment, is moved to sorting tables where workers remove any that don't look top tier. Land of a Thousand Hills only selects the highest-grade coffee beans, which are placed on drying tables until they reach 12 percent humidity and are then stored for shipment.

Whenever I visit one of our coffee washing stations, I marvel at all the sights and sounds of the place. A lady of almost ninety years carries a basket of coffee cherries on her head alongside other farmers. Water gurgles, diesel motors roar, and the rat-tat-tat of the washing machine serenades me. Children stick their heads in the door and shout, "*Muzungu! Muzungu!*" which means "white man." As I approach them, they pet my hairy arms and tell me I look like a gorilla. Rwandese men do not have hair on their arms, so for these kids to see a man who is white and has hairy arms is a rarity.

Though Bukonya was one of the regions hit worst by the genocide, hope is breaking through.

I've been working with the Rwandan people for the last ten years, and I'm amazed by what God has accomplished, both in that country and through our company. I'm grateful for the friendships I've forged and opportunities to partner with those friends to create jobs, craft high-quality coffee, and cultivate good. If I lived a hundred lifetimes, I'd never be able to express adequate gratitude for being able to play a miniscule role in the hope-giving transformation of Rwanda.

But my journey to Bukonya began years earlier with a simple invitation to accept my calling.

The Shore of God's Grace

I was raised in a fundamentalist Baptist church, even though my grandfather was an orthodox Jew. (The dynamic created some interesting conversations about Jesus.)

In my church, following Jesus emphasized a list of dos and don'ts, but my youth pastor, Ron, was a stabilizing voice. He gave me permission to speak freely, and I felt comfortable sharing my deepest doubts and fears with him. I had a rebellious streak and was trying to flesh out who I was and what I believed. Without him, I might have walked away from the faith.

As high school graduation approached, a lot of my friends urged me to become a pastor, but when I was accepted to Cedarville College, I decided to major in psychology instead. I didn't know many pastors I wanted to be like.

While I continued to wrestle with my faith in college, I was trying to be authentic and enjoy life. I wanted to take a break from the rigid religion of my upbringing. I still believed in God, mentored youth in our town, and visited old people in the nursing home, but I dumped the oppressive list of rules. I wanted to explore life and find out what I really believed. This led to drinking some beer, smoking some pot, and waking up with a few headaches. Many a night my friends and I would go camping and around the fire talk of life and what it really meant to be on adventure with God.

After college I considered seminary but decided to pursue a master's degree in psychology instead. I felt I could have a greater impact on people through one-on-one relationships. I can't explain how exactly, but during that time I felt God pulling me back to himself. It was like the tide of my soul was coming back in to the shore of God's grace. I began to explore the gifts and passions God had buried deep inside me while at the same time realizing that life was messy. I encountered a lot of people with a lot of pain.

After completing graduate school, I started a private practice in counseling and soon began to focus on industrial psychology. I realized that the same things that made people effective or

ineffective personally made them effective and ineffective professionally. I found myself working with CEOs of large companies,
entrepreneurs, pastors, and teams to help them discover and
live their callings. In my practice I implemented a program
called Lifeswork, which focused on helping people find their
aim, purpose, and pursuit in life, that which best demonstrates
to the world their uniqueness and reason for living. Through
the Lifeswork process I was blessed to witness thousands of
individuals discover their callings and future career goals.

I was successful, but I wasn't completely at peace. Helping
people was fulfilling, but the corporate rat race was maddening.
I wondered how much long-term impact I was having. I was
leading people to discover their "Lifeswork," but I felt mine
was in transition. I decided to take myself through the same
process I used with others.

While hiking the coastal path in Cornwall, England, I prayed,
hiked, thought, and leaned in to considering my own calling. I
clarified and wrote down my primary proficiencies: teaching,
preaching, idea creation, and coaching. Then I asked how I
might apply these gifts effectively. I thought about my purpose
and crystalized my passions.

"Maybe now is the time to become a pastor," I thought.

I had been preaching one to two Sundays a month at a Men-
nonite church, and I felt alive when I stood behind the pulpit.
The path I wasn't sure I'd ever actually pursue seemed to be the
one God was leading me toward. A few years later, I pursued
ordination within the Anglican Communion, became a priest,
and planted St. Peter's Place Anglican Church, a church focused
on building supernatural community among people mired in
life's messiness. But I still felt like God had something more
for me, perhaps another adventure.

"God, if you want to invite me to more, I will run with it," I prayed.

At an Anglican conference, God's "more" came. I met Bishop John Rucyahana of Rwanda, a man who was firmly planted in the church but was also working with businesses throughout his country to restore the genocide-ravaged economy.

"Bishop, you seem to have one foot in the church and one foot in the marketplace," I said.

"No, my brother," Rucyahana responded. "I have both feet in the Bible."

"How can our churches help you?" I asked.

He paused.

"We have good coffee."

The wheels in my mind began to spin. I wondered what would happen if people of faith here in the United States drank a coffee that matched the message they preached on Sundays. It was just an inkling, but that seed would yield good fruit in only a handful of years.

A few months later, I ordered twenty sacks of Rwandan coffee and a roaster off eBay. A year later, I had a fully functioning coffee company forging partnerships with churches, Christian conferences, and coffee connoisseurs who want the drink they love to make a difference in the lives of others.

Rwanda is nicknamed the "land of a thousand hills," which seemed a perfect name for the venture. We were using coffee to bring restoration and reconciliation to a people who needed it. I found myself wanting to "be me and do good." I'd always been a person with a variety of interests. Some called me the consummate Renaissance man. Having been involved in counseling, consulting, a bit of construction, the church, and now coffee, I was excited to realize that this new mission or calling might be big enough to tie in all of my varied interests.

Our tagline said it all: "Drink Coffee. Do Good."

Myths We Believe

There is a lot of talk about "calling" these days, but my experiences have taught me that much of it is mythical. As I learned to follow the inkling I believe God gave me, I had to dispel five prevalent myths that threaten to keep us all from discovering our callings.

Myth #1: "My Job Is My Calling"

The concept of a job is relatively new. The word *job* comes from the old English word *jobbe*, which means a part or a piece. Before the industrial era, a job was a temporary task someone did. You might go help someone with a job like building a barn or painting a fence or planting corn. But then you'd go back to doing what you were born into—like working on your farm with your family.

The onset of the industrial age in the late 1700s changed this. People were leaving their lives to work a job, which became a means of achieving an income that was distinct from one's life. Suddenly, they weren't just "John" or "Sally" but rather "John, the coal miner" or "Sally, the factory worker." What we did suddenly became the defining part of who we were as human beings. Both Matthew Smith in *The Reinvention of Work* and Erich Fromm in *To Have or To Be* have described the significance of this transition.

If you try to find all of your meaning or purpose in something you do from 9:00 until 5:00, you'll be disappointed. And you'll also feel shipwrecked if you get laid off because your job has become your identity. We need to remember that our life's work is more than our job. One's calling is more than what one gets paid to do.

Myth #2: "My Task List Is My Calling"

In a goal-oriented society that places a premium on productivity, it's easy to believe that what we get done or what we have to get done is our calling. We may even try to program life into a set of enumerated items that must be achieved and draw a sense of fulfillment from how much we accomplish. Seeing calling this way boils it down to something that can be controlled and keeps us from creating. It also robs us of the ability to create since we overlook what might be because we're focused on what is.

You may have been told you were supposed to go to college or get married and have children. Or you've been told that you should pursue a career that makes money so you can save up for retirement. Suddenly that task list becomes your purpose for living. But calling is more than the obligations we've accepted or been given.

Myth #3: "My Calling Must Be Grandiose"

We live in a time where success stories and sensational narratives are splashed all over the internet. A Christian conference draws tens of thousands or a group of middle school students raises a large sum of cash to fight slavery. As a result, we've come to believe that this must be what following our calling should look like, that we must have some grand, "God-sized" plan. So we start to dream up the biggest, sexiest, flashiest, most dramatic goal we can.

This myth has been popularized by wide-eyed Western Christians who love celebrity and success. But most people don't have monumental callings. In fact, they're an idea that most Christians throughout history have been baffled by.

Mother Teresa's calling may have opened some big doors for her, but the majority of her life was spent doing things that would make most of our stomachs turn. It wasn't sexy or flashy. And of course, most of the Mother Teresas in this life are never recognized or celebrated on a large stage or in front of network news cameras. We must remember that faithfulness is often effective but not usually dramatic.

Myth #4: "My Calling Means Doing One Thing for the Rest of My Life"

This myth will often paralyze someone who is searching for purpose. It's hard to commit when you assume it's a once-for-all-time decision. But most people know instinctively that this isn't the way calling works. A modern college graduate, for example, can expect to live in various places, pursue a range of goals, and have several careers throughout his or her life.

Since calling is more than a job, when you clarify your calling, you may find many ways to live that out. I've been a professor at a university, an executive coach, a church pastor, and a social entrepreneur. These have all been legitimate ways to express my calling. We must remember that calling isn't a life sentence.

Myth #5: "Ministry Is a Higher Calling"

The idea that we have to enter into full-time ministry to serve God is a sham. (I don't know a softer way to say this.) I've heard many pastors talk about Christ's calling Peter to "Come, follow me" and center in on the fact that Peter "left his nets" to become Jesus's disciple. Many of us have been taught that Peter left his work—that he used to be a fisherman, but when he became a Jesus follower, he became something else. The implicit message is that fishing (or any other venture) is okay, but full-time ministry is better.

If you keep reading the New Testament, you'll find that after the crucifixion, Peter went back to fishing. He may have left his net for a time, but he never sold his boat. When Jesus was on the shore after the resurrection, the disciples were fishing again without much success. Peter's call teaches us that we must love Christ more than our work, not that we must leave our work.

This myth almost kept me from founding a for-profit coffee business. I almost decided to do coffee as a ministry of the church, which probably would have stunted its growth. As a priest, I could have felt like I had already reached the pinnacle of calling. Surely, God didn't have anything else for me in addition to pastoring. But God does not have to call you away from who you are and who you've been. As with Peter, who we are and what we do are woven together in the fabric of our callings. I was a creator and starter before pastoring and still am today.

1. If you've not yet discovered your calling, that particular expression of you *being you* and *doing good*, what do you think has held you back?

2. As you consider Jonathan's journey, what resonates with your own, and what strikes you as being most different from your own?

3. Right now, what is one "next step" you could take?

- 2 -

Never Again, Again

Be Who You Are

His name was Heimann Goldstein, but most people called him Jack. He was a stocky Jewish man, short and gruff with olive skin, who called pre–World War II England his home. Jack was a haberdasher, a peddler who sold bits of cloth, needles, thread, and sundries as he walked from village to village discovering what people needed. Each Friday, he would travel to the north end of London to make his purchases, hurrying home just before dusk to begin his Sabbath rest.

Jack was known for his cheerful trademark yodeling and the sound of loose coins jingling in his pockets that announced his arrival. He found a way to work hard and to take what he had and do good in a land where he never quite felt welcomed. It seems he learned this art of working hard and doing good from his father, a tailor who made clothing for the czars of Russia prior to the Bolshevic Revolution, escaping to England under the threat of death.

Jack enjoyed an occasional pint at the pub, trying to forget the atrocities happening to his people in other parts of Europe. One evening while at home, Jack received word that a Jewish girl had been thrown through a plate glass window at the pub he knew well. Jack and his son rushed to the establishment to help the girl and teach the bullies a lesson. The violence on this girl was personal to them and they refused to overlook it. That was just the kind of man Jack was—one who helped others, perhaps at times without thinking.

Knowing "Pop"

But to me Heimann "Jack" Goldstein was more than a good man and a product of his time; he was my grandfather. He changed his family name to "Golden" prior to the Great War because of anti-Semitism in England. I grew up hearing stories of his adventures with my father and uncles, and it shaped my strong sense of pride in my heritage.

I was born as an American citizen in Valparaiso, Indiana, and raised Baptist, but I was always proud of the Jewish blood in my veins. I wore a Star of David around my neck in high school. And when my sister married a Jewish man, I felt pride when they initiated the Hava Nagila dance at their wedding. As a teenager, I'd think of my granddad—"Pop," as I called him—when I read books by Elie Wiesel and novels by Chaim Potok.

I imagined that if it were not for my great-grandfather's escape to England in the 1890s, the thread of my life might have been woven into the horrible Holocaust. I envisioned being part of a Jewish resistance force in the Warsaw Ghetto who with stealth fought against the Nazis and protected innocents for many months. I imagined hiding in the woods like one of Potok's characters, trying to escape.

I visited my granddad every few years growing up. His voice was deep and raspy, indicative of the pipe he loved to smoke. He didn't talk a lot, but when he did, he never spoke of war. With a gleam in his eye, he would ask if I wanted to see his helicopter in the back garden. As timing would have it, every time I ran to the back, the helicopter was out on a trip. It was our little joke.

How I wish it were possible to sit down with Pop today and have a pint of Guinness at my own favorite pub. I'd ask my grandfather all the adult questions my childhood mind never thought of. I would quiz him about his work, his struggles, his joys, how he made a living and even more importantly a life. I'd share how my calling has been crafted, and we would both be amazed to learn how our stories are woven together.

Hutus, Tutsis, and a Brutal Legacy

In 1994 Rwanda's thousand hills of peace became littered with death. The Interahamwe of the militant Hutu regime slaughtered more than one million ethnic Tutsis in just one hundred days. Neighbor turned against neighbor, Christian against Christian, and in some cases, husband against wife. The seeds of dissension had been growing in this tiny east African country about the size of the state of Maryland since the Belgium priests had "Christianized" the country.

After World War I, when the Belgium Catholic priests arrived, they found a country with three ethnic groups who lived in peace and had intermarried for generations. The ethnic Hutus were mostly farmers, the Twas were a pigmy group who were short in stature and workers of clay, and the Tutsis were cattle ranchers and the ethnic group of the royal family. The Belgians, who knew little of a collaborative society, elevated the roles of the Tutsis, minimized the roles of the Hutus, and handed out ID cards. It didn't matter if your family was both Hutu and Tutsi; the Belgians forced identification and classified you based on your looks. The seeds of strife were planted.

In the 1950s, power shifted to the Hutus as the Belgium priests influenced by Marxism started empowering the Hutus instead of the Tutsis. This led to the first genocide in the 1950s when many Tutsis fled the country in exile to Uganda, Tanzania, and the Congo. During the next forty years with the Hutu in government control, the Tutsis were discriminated against, but the land was relatively peaceful. But in the 1990s, discrimination escalated to violence erupting in a catastrophic genocide when the Hutu powers used the government and media to enact a brutal campaign against Tutsi citizens.

As much as 10 percent of the Rwandan population was decimated, by some estimates. For the first time in modern history, an army was raised within an army. The children of ethnic Tutsis raised in Uganda who were serving in the Ugandan military crossed country boundaries, changed their uniforms, and rescued their brethren, but not before a million were murdered.

Since then, the country has been learning to thrive again. Development is strong, reconciliation is palpable, and the Rwandan people have become leaders in demonstrating what can happen when repentance and forgiveness are engaged.

I was intrigued to learn that the Tutsis were practicing Jews prior to the influence of the West. Europeans called them the

"Golden People" because of their Hasidic features. The Tutsis were often referred to as the Tutsi-Jews because they traced their lineage back to Jews in Ethiopia. I have a picture in my office of an old Rwandan Tutsi farmer bringing his coffee cherries to market, and he looks a lot like my dad. After the Holocaust, the world said, "Never again." But in 1994, the world sat back and watched it happen again when Rwanda experienced their own holocaust.

Today, when I visit Rwanda and do the Hava Nagila in the dance circles, I can't help being swept with awe at how God has woven together my story with my calling. God has led me to confront something that is surprisingly connected with who I am. As I've reflected on the way my story connects with the story of Rwanda, I'm amazed by the similarities.

But maybe I shouldn't be.

Made to Be Fully Who We Are

Christians claim to believe not only in God but also in a God who is involved. We worship a God who sees us, loves us, interacts with us. We serve a God who is concerned with the affairs of men and women. And if we believe in an involved God, we must also believe our stories are not accidental.

Every human with a beating heart is more than bone and flesh. He or she is also a living narrative, a character in a real-life drama unfolding on planet Earth. Our life stories are a cosmic collaboration cowritten by God and by us. Yet when we determine to write new chapters in our lives, we don't often consider the stories we've been writing with God until now. So we become living narratives that are disconnected from who we are, where we've been, and what we've become.

The first secret to discovering our callings is to look at our talents, our knowledge areas, our skills, and our past. It is to see our lives as a story, to read it, and to be who you are.

When my children were young, I struggled to play little kids' games with them for extended periods of time. Those who know me can attest that I "don't do board games." As a young dad I would get bored with Monopoly, and I felt guilty for it. But what I thought was a problem turned out to be the logical end of who I am. I'm an adventurer, and I don't like sitting indoors on a rug for hours on end, moving a game piece. I was trying to express myself apart from myself.

One day, I decided to change the way I interacted with my kids. I began inviting them with me to venture into the woods, pretend we were pirates, knock down old trees, or go trudging through creeks. We created elaborate challenges together. I built a mud pit one year, and they jousted over it like medieval knights. I bought tree-climbing gear, and we learned to scale heights together, hanging dozens of feet in the air. Once my kids came home to find a note saying their mother had been "kidnapped" and we needed to find her. We followed the clues, found the map, and made our way to the hotel where the "kidnapper" said we would find her. We went to the room where my wife said, "Surprise!"

Parenting my children in this way taught me something about my calling: I need to be who I am in order to do what I need to do. When I am fully me, I am the best dad possible, just as it makes me the best entrepreneur possible.

Why We Choose What We Do

As I've worked to help others find their callings, I've discovered that most people pursue a vocation for one of at least five reasons:

- **The vocation sounds interesting.** A lot of people become teachers or nurses or scientists because it seems intriguing. This reason is particularly common among college students who don't know what they want to do but are forced to choose a major and life path anyway.

- **The vocation appears heroic.** As we've become more socially conscious, many people desire to do something that sounds noble. They want their work to "matter" or "count," so they pursue nonprofit or church work. Usually, these individuals find out that those jobs feel a lot less heroic than they seem from the outside.

- **The vocation seems lucrative.** A good friend of mine decided upon entering college that he wanted to become a doctor. His motivation wasn't that he loved science or medicine or serving others. He knew that doctors made a lot of money, and that seemed like a good enough reason. After getting his degree in biology, he was burned out and depressed. He ended up finding his true calling—one connected to passions he'd nurtured but overlooked his entire life—and today is a journalist. Too many people attempt to live life with only money in mind.

- **The vocation pleases others.** Many people pursue a path in life because someone else told them they should or because others pressure them into doing it. How many people attend law school because their parents pushed them there? How many end up running the family business, not because they want to, but because they feel like they should? The opinions of others matter, but when we fail to consider whether or not our own story is intertwined with the narrative we're writing, we should beware.

- **The vocation is not a call but a covet.** Sometimes we do something because we want what another has or does rather than cultivating a calling out of our own identity. I recently descended into a tailspin because another coffee company secured an account with a national fast food chain that we were courting. I wanted what the other company had. But one's calling should be born independently of our desires to be someone else or have the lives and opportunities of others.

These are some of the counterfit calls that we respond to. I want you to know, though, that God wants to call *you* to himself and wants you to do good with him. He wants you as a co-creator to make this world a better place, but you can only do that when you avoid the counterfeit calls and embrace all of who you are.

God Uses All of You

In John 21, the risen Christ is standing on the shore while Peter is fishing. This hadn't been a particularly successful day for Peter, but when the man on the beach tells him to cast his nets on the other side, he listens. Suddenly, Peter's nets are filled to overflowing. I find it interesting that Jesus decided to bless Peter's work with one of his final miracles.

When Peter finally gets back to shore with a heap of fish, Jesus looks at the flopping pile of fish—153 to be exact—and says, "Peter, do you love me more than these?" Peter replies, "Yes, Lord. You know I love you" (see John 21:15). After three rounds of questioning, Jesus tells Peter to feed his sheep. Christ met Peter in the midst of his work when he first called him, and Jesus blessed his work on one of the darkest days of Peter's life. Jesus didn't tell Peter to leave his work but instead to use his work, his fishing, as a means of doing good and living out ministry. You don't have to leave what you love to do in order to follow the call. In fact your call may be just what you are doing, perhaps fishing—just do it as a means to help others.

The fascinating exchange teaches us something incredible about our own callings. Jesus is not saying we must forsake or ignore our stories to follow him but rather that we must love him more than our work. Rather than scorn Peter's love of fishing, Jesus was asking, "Will you let me help coauthor the rest of this story?"

Rather than pursue a calling or vocation for a fleeting reason— because it seems interesting or heroic or lucrative or obligatory or desirable—we must begin by taking stock of our stories. What are the most significant events of your life that have shaped you? Which experiences have made you uniquely you? Is there something about the life you've lived that gnaws at you, excites you, or shakes you to your core?

Until we stop running from who we are; until we stop pursuing rules, roles, and responsibilities; until we take stock of who we are and the great stories God has been writing with us, we cannot begin to pursue our callings.

As we discover our stories and who God has been shaping us into, we need to accept our failings and imperfections. I was traveling recently, and I asked a member of my church to preach in my absence. He has an incredible gift for understanding and communicating Scripture, but he hasn't preached in a decade. Upon my asking, he told me that after his second divorce, he felt like God put him on the shelf. He stopped having his morning reflective time, shortened his prayers, and felt his relationship with God had diminished.

"Maybe God hasn't put you on that shelf," I responded. "Perhaps you've put yourself there."

I asked him if his failing was bigger than God's grace. He said no, God was bigger. And the following Sunday, he stood in our church to preach.

If God is coauthoring our stories, we can rest assured that nothing will shipwreck the narrative. God never gets writer's block. He can use the tragedies and comedies and dramas that befall us and that we help create. Too many people sit on life's sidelines and fail to live courageously because they believe they've been damaged. We've never considered that God may see more in us than our past and our sins and our foibles. God can overcome what you've snorted or who you've slept with or what you've stolen or who you've hurt.

When God decides to take you, God takes all of you. This doesn't mean we don't attempt to live better lives, but rather that God wants to take us on an adventure despite it all. Paul was a dictatorial Pharisee, and then he became a somewhat dictatorial Christian. Jacob was a trickster before and after God found him. Peter was impulsive and reckless his entire ministry.

When we are on the precipice of discovering our callings, we often begin making excuses.

"I'm not talented enough." Too often we feel called to a task but not equipped to make it work. My experience has been that hard work is as integral to success as raw talent. Remember that if you're connecting your calling to your story, it will spring from a place of your greatest talents.

"I'm not smart enough." If you don't think you are smart enough to live out your calling, I have good news for you.

We live in the internet age when generations of knowledge are available at our fingertips. You may not know everything, but you can learn. And you can surround yourself with people who are stronger where you are weaker. Only intelligent people question whether they are smart enough to begin with; it's the stupid ones who fail to take stock of what they do not yet know.

"I'm not wealthy enough." Some of the greatest world changers in history were not wealthy. An idea injected with passion is often more powerful than a great fortune. Do you know what the Wright Brothers, Amazon, Hewlett-Packard, Disney, Mattel, and many of the greatest bands of the last century have in common?[1] They all started in a garage. If you're financially limited, get creative and start small. Even the biggest pine tree begins as a small seed.

"I'm not holy enough." This is a lie that Christians in particular tell ourselves. It's an odd one, when you think about it, because the Bible is a record of unholy people used by God to do amazing things. Almost every person in both Testaments (with the exception of Jesus, of course) has near-fatal flaws—from Moses the murderer to Samson the rule breaker, David the adulterer, and Peter the denier. If you think you're not "holy enough," rest easy. You're in good company.

If we allow ourselves to tell and believe these lies, they create one of the greatest hurdles to discovering our callings: shame.

As shame expert Brené Brown says, "Owning our story can be hard but not nearly as difficult as spending our lives running from it. Embracing our vulnerabilities is risky but not nearly as dangerous as giving up on love and belonging and joy—the experiences that make us the most vulnerable. Only when we are brave enough to explore the darkness will we discover the infinite power of our light."[2]

The hard part of struggling with calling is that you are involved. If it were just a job, it wouldn't matter as much. But when *you* are what is at stake, it becomes painful, risky, and difficult. When you integrate who you are with what you do, you have nowhere to run. You're naked and defenseless when it all hits the fan. So taking who you are and accepting it, offering it, and using it takes courage. But it is worth it.

Throw off the lies you're telling yourself and make peace with the shadows in your story. Only then can you step into the light of your calling.

Work as the Fabric of This World

The apocryphal wisdom book of Ecclesiasticus, also known as Sirach, is a powerful resource of wisdom, commentary, and instruction that was well known in the times of the early church. The book is accepted as part of the biblical canon by Catholic and Eastern Orthodox churches, and Lutherans and Anglicans also include readings from it in their lectionaries.

In the thirty-eighth chapter of this sage writing, we're given descriptions of workers who pour their lives into their work:

> Without them no city can be inhabited,
>> and wherever they live, they will not go hungry.
> Yet they are not sought out for the council of the people,
>> nor do they attain eminence in the public assembly.
> They do not sit in the judge's seat,
>> nor do they understand the decisions of the courts;

they cannot expound discipline or judgment,
    and they are not found among the rulers.
But they maintain the fabric of the world,
    and their concern is for the exercise of their trade.

                        Sirach 38:32–34 NRSV

It is cool to think that the very fabric of this world is maintained by my work and your work. The history of the world is like a fabric weaved by artisans of the Almighty. Your story and mine and the work we engage in are being knitted into this fabric, imbuing it with color and texture and beauty. When we seek out our callings, we don't begin from scratch. God has been weaving with us since the day we were born. The fabric we're producing has a history, and it is enmeshed with other stories and histories all around us.

I've always felt like a wanderer and fighter anyway, but knowing my history and my family's story helped me make sense of it. The stories of anti-Semitism told to me by my dad and my uncle Harry formed a lens through which I see injustice and oppression. Because of my own family's story, I try to live and work in a redemptive fashion, taking a stand for those who are oppressed. The stories of my grandfather's hard work and the way he stood up for people, brought joy to others, and applied his trade informs my work in Rwanda today. Part of our calling is connecting with those things that God engraves on our heart from an early age and agreeing to start working and weaving with the fabric we've been given.

I'm sure my Pop had no idea that the stories he'd pass on, the experiences he lived, and even the act of defending a little Jewish girl brutalized by anti-Semites would be woven into a story of redemption and reconciliation on another continent among the people of Rwanda. I think if that burly, pipe-smoking fighter were around today to see the work of Land of a Thousand Hills, he'd be proud.

1. What life events have made you uniquely you?
2. Is there a particular experience you've lived that gnaws at you, excites you, or shakes you to your core?
3. Right now, what is one "next step" you could take?

– 3 –

A Mechanic in Mexico

Use What You Have

During one of the happiest times of my life, I'd often drive home from work covered in coke.

No, I didn't have an affinity for the white powder.

During the summers of my high school and college years I worked for my dad's company, L. B. Golden Inc. Pipefitting & Construction, the coke ovens of Bethlehem Steel in Portage, Indiana. Coke is a fuel, usually made from coal, that has few impurities and high carbon content. It burns extremely hot and is used in the steelmaking process. In July of 1993, my job was to run new gas lines in the ovens.

On the campus of Bethlehem Steel, large smokestacks several hundred feet in diameter stretched to the sky. Corrugated steel buildings several football fields in size opened and closed their massive doors to swallow, and then eject, mammoth shipping trucks. Though framed by the backdrop of scenic Lake Michigan, the busy mill was rough and dirty.

The coke ovens were the heart of this aggressive industrial plant. Coal was heated to over one thousand degrees to produce pure coke, which was then used in the "blast furnace" where iron was forged.

Each morning at 6:00 a.m. I reported to my foreman, Bobby. At sixty-five, Bobby looked like a hobo with salt-and-pepper hair, a three-day growth of beard, and a playful twinkle in his eyes. Bobby and I started each day together next to a weathered wooden workbench with a couple cups of black coffee and two powdered-sugar donuts. Between bites, Bobby would flatten out the rolled blueprints mapping out the day's work.

After gathering the requisite materials from one of my dad's trucks—usually six-foot lengths of various gauge pipe, industrial wrenches, welding rods, and handheld blowtorches—we'd labor all day in the belly of the dirty, sooty coke ovens. During breaks, we sat together on coolers to discuss weighty world affairs, like the Steelers' unexpected loss to the Cowboys.

On a typical day I'd consume about a loaf's worth of sandwiches. When the whistle blew at 5:00 to release us, I would stand, blanketed in soot, and survey the pipe we'd constructed, pleased with the welds we'd made. Driving home beside my dad on the bench seat of his '76 Ford pickup, I was filthy, exhausted, and happy.

The next day I'd get up with the sun and do it all again.

Bobby was a second cousin of country singing legend Johnny Cash and shared Cash's gritty, earthy approach to life. In addition to working for my dad as a pipe fitter, Bobby held down jobs as a truck driver and Pentecostal pastor. In his free time, Bobby moonlighted as a missionary to Mexico.

Working shoulder to shoulder one day after lunch, as I was sweating off a few of those sandwiches I'd just consumed, Bobby shared a bit of his story with me. After becoming a Christian at sixteen, he took a mission trip to Mexico where he worked alongside a long-term missionary named Vincent. Bobby was captivated by the way Vincent was living his life.

As they laid bricks together, not entirely unlike my own apprenticeship under Bobby, Bobby gushed to Vincent, "I wish God would use me to do something important for his church by preaching the gospel. But I haven't been to college or Bible school."

With tears in his eyes, Vincent said, "I wish I had a dozen men like you, Bobby—mechanics, bricklayers, welders who'd build bridges and provide water as they lived out the gospel."

Bobby explained to me that the next summer he built a bridge for this Mexican community. And when he discovered they needed school supplies and medicines and clothing, he asked for donations from his friends and area churches. At the end of the year, he began loading a semitrailer full of supplies, and every Christmas, he drove down to share them with the village.

Bobby didn't wait to respond to God's call until he'd donned a black gown, grasped an impressive diploma, and tossed his graduation cap into the air. (If he had, he might never have made it back to Mexico!) No, Bobby courageously responded to God's call by using what he had. People like Bobby, who live in response to God's call in the present, wrangle the courage to respond with what they have. Believing that it is enough, they move forward with the tools, training, money, and relationships they already possess.

One Brave Step

I've become convinced that the reason most great works aren't achieved and most callings aren't fulfilled is not because we fail to engage—rather, we lack the courage to take the first step. We bumble weak excuses about not having the right training or tools. We balk because we believe we don't know the right people. Or we put off the first step until the funds materialize. But what you have right now is enough to do what God's calling you to do.

On a sweltering day in a small village in Mexico, Bobby realized he already had the tools he needed to respond to God's call. And the same is true when you take your first brave step.

Perhaps you've been postponing doing what you know you were made to do until after graduation. Or you've been waiting on just the right business or ministry partner—who will compensate for your weaknesses—to knock on your front door and introduce herself. You might be waiting until after you have kids, or perhaps you've got the kids and are planning to launch after they're grown and out of the house. When they finish college. Or when you're retired.

What you are being called to do right now is take one brave step.

One step.

The first time I hired a salesperson for my coaching and consulting business, which I was operating out of the screened porch of my apartment, it felt like a monumental financial commitment. At the time, it was.

Phil was doing some legwork in the community when I gave him a call on his first day of work.

"Hey, Phil. How are the calls going? Any good prospects yet?"

"Um." He hesitated. "I'm in downtown Atlanta on Peachtree Street. The Chamber of Commerce is closed, so I can't get a list of area businesses for three days."

What I heard in Phil's cautious response was that he assumed I'd be paying him to "wait around" for three days. I'm pretty sure that my eyes spun around like a slot machine and smoke poured out of my ears like on an old-school Warner Brothers cartoon. Attempting to cork my rage, I diplomatically asked Phil if he'd ever heard of a phone book. Then I encouraged him to start calling immediately!

Two weeks later, Phil was searching for other employment. Not because his calling didn't match with the assignment, but because he was not willing to use what he had to get the job done.

Crafting Beautiful Work with an Ugly Knife

During a recent trip to Rwanda, I glimpsed the most holy expression of this foundational principle. Bumping along the dusty road between Musanze and Kigali, we pulled over at a local craft cooperative for my guests to peruse peace baskets, wood carvings, and other Rwandan hand crafts. It's a favorite stop of mine on the now familiar journey, and the staff have come to know me well. Wandering around back, I chatted with some of the talented wood carvers as my friends perused the merchandise.

Noticing various artisans in different stages of the carving process, I watched these women and men transform raw blocks of wood into miniature elephants and giraffes as well as pieces for a board game called Igisoro. When I applauded their work— I literally clapped my hands in praise—Josef, one of the men who'd been squatting as he worked, stood up to show me the knife he was using. The tool was about fifty years old, rusted where the blade met the handle, chipped and worn with age. The craftsman's family's livelihood depended upon his work at the rural cooperative, and he asked me if it would be possible to bring him new carving tools on my next trip. It seemed a reasonable request.

But what I love about Josef is that he didn't allow the absence of the right tool to keep him from doing the work before him.

Other times, I've seen folks wait for the right training. These men and women wait for some time in the future—when they're gripping a degree, or have mastered another language, or have been certified as experts—in order to move into the calling to which God has been wooing them. And while it's probable that you will continue to acquire new competencies that will further equip you to embrace your calling, you can embrace it right now.

Perhaps your one brave step will be as simple as researching folks who are excellent at what you're being called to do.

Or maybe you'll purchase a blank sketchbook where you'll begin to record fresh ideas and sketch prototypes.

Your one brave step may be to call in favors so you can shadow an expert for a day.

Every calling begins with one brave step.

Courage to Begin

Years ago, I sat in my office in the historic downtown of Roswell, Georgia, with a new career coaching client. Julie was a young woman in her twenties who had been working as a teacher at a local community college for about three years. An inkling that she was called to be a missionary to South America had driven her to my office. It had become the deepest longing of her heart.

Roswell has become increasingly diverse over the last decade or two, and during the season Julie and I were working together, the city had a rich population of Mexican and South American immigrants. Recognizing a unique opportunity, I queried, "Have you invited any of your neighbors into your home? Have you found opportunities to share the gospel with the folks who are living around you?"

Her expression was blank.

Julie confessed that she hadn't spoken to any of them. But then her countenance changed as she began to understand where I was headed.

"If ministering to South American people is really your calling, why aren't you doing it right where you are?"

I've discovered that if something is a person's life's work, she finds a way to work at it where she is, with what she has.

Jesus repeatedly told his friends that the kingdom of God was near. He didn't say, "It's coming in the distant future!" He announced that it was near. Possibly as near as the Bolivian immigrant standing behind us in the grocery store checkout line. Many of us are tempted to dream about a different future without recognizing that what's even better news is that we're called to a different present. And this present informs that future we envision, because the buildings of tomorrow are built on the foundations of today.

To assign God's will and calling on our lives to the future relieves us of the responsibility of acting today. If most of us were more honest, we might tweak the Lord's Prayer to read, "Thy kingdom come, thy will be done, when we die and go to heaven." But Jesus wants his kingdom to come on earth *today* as it is in heaven. What my foreman Bobby discovered was that all of our work is a means of making God's world on earth a bit more like heaven.

This isn't to say that you won't ever need more training. If you're called to be my heart surgeon, you'll need quite a bit of schooling. But you can still be an instrument of healing today—as an assistant on a medical mission trip or a hospital volunteer. All you need to start working is courage.

A Tribute to Brave, Foolhardy Launches

My dad enlisted in the military to fight in World War II when he was sixteen. The war ended when he was twenty, and he interviewed for a job at the docks in St. Austell, England. Though he'd never picked up a welding rod or donned a welding mask in his life, when the interviewing foreman asked him if he knew how to weld, my dad stretched the truth, believed in the future, and said yes. He needed the job and believed that he'd learn fast enough.

The rhythm of creation that unfolds in Genesis is not unlike my dad's "creative" visioning. God speaks matter into existence with words. Then when God surveys what has been created, he blesses it with words. Because words are so powerful—both divine and human ones—we have to be careful about what we say we can or can't do. By the time the thought in our mind escapes our lips, we've agreed to it twice! If you are meant to do something, you'll speak it and you'll do it.

I'd been dating my now-wife for almost four years when my old college roommate, Larry, who'd been wed for three years, asked me if I was ever going to marry Brenda.

We were sharing a Guinness at a local pub when Larry asked pointedly, "So, what are you waiting for?"

I had an answer for that. And a good one.

"I'll marry her," I assured him. "When I save enough money, I'm going to propose." I was secretly pleased at my thoughtful response.

Larry, seemingly oblivious to the evident wisdom, burst out laughing. "Bro, you will never have enough money."

A few weeks later I emptied my bank account at Botany Bay Florist. As I pointed to six dozen roses and various other flowers, the florist asked me what I had done wrong.

"Surely it wasn't that bad," she quipped.

Prying Brenda's hidden apartment key out from behind the floor molding in the hallway, I snuck in before she was due to return home from work. After lining the stairway with flowers and filling her living room with a trail of rose petals, I waited out of sight for her to arrive home from work.

When her own key clicked in the lock, I heard Brenda crack the door and inch into her fragrant apartment. Following the rose petal trail, she turned the corner into the living room where I'd been waiting.

Dropping down on one knee, I bumbled the words that had been rattling around in my head for days, "Brenda Elizabeth Rose, will you do me the honor of being my wife?"

Weeping, she gasped, "What do you think?"

"I don't know." I grinned. "That's why I'm asking."

Brenda took the brave risk of saying yes and agreed to join this penniless suitor in the crazy adventure of life. I'd learned from Larry, in the most wonderful way, the importance of following the call whether or not the money's in the bank.

If we wait until we have enough money to do what's important, we almost never will.

Failure to Launch

Years later, a businessman named Mark would remind me of that life-changing lesson I'd learned from my roommate

Larry—the one about waiting for a magical time in the future to act. Mark, the CFO for a large tech company, came to me for coaching because he was no longer happy in his lucrative work. As he and I worked through the coaching program I created,[3] stories of Mark's passions unfolded, and it became clear that his life's work did not include working as a CFO. Mark had a hunger to build something, to be a craftsman. He loved carpentry, had dabbled in some projects around his home, and wanted to spend his days building quality custom furniture.

As we drafted a plan, Mark explained that when he had enough money he would quit his job and pursue his dream, a logic with which I was all too familiar. When I asked him how much he would need in the bank, he estimated that what he'd need to feel secure enough to take the leap would be one million dollars.

A number of months went by before I saw Mark again. When we caught up, he had well over a million bucks in reserve. The time was ripe. But when I asked if he was ready to take the next step, he backpedaled. Cautious, he told me that he'd changed his mind and needed closer to two million.

The problem with erecting requisite hurdles to cross before responding to God's call is that there will always be more requirements. Mark, in my opinion, had made money his god when it became the voice he heeded and obeyed. In the book of Isaiah, God is pretty ticked at the Israelites for not listening to and following his call: "You spread the table for fortune and you mixed the wine for destiny" (see Isa. 65:11). They'd been hosting a communion service of sorts for the neighboring nations' false gods whose names were Fortune and Destiny. Though I haven't, and Mark hasn't, bowed to wooden idols dedicated to ancient near eastern gods, I admit that I have listened to the voices of fortune and destiny, planned accordingly, and lived out a prayer of sorts in their homage. And they're not even good gods. They tend to be fickle, are often absent, and always seem to demand more from me than I've given them. If you wait to run after God's purpose for your life until you have enough money, you'll never launch, and you may even be serving a false god.

I Got By with a Little Help from My Friends

When I'm not in Rwanda or traveling in the United States, I spend most of my time in my 1830s house-turned-office in the Roswell Mill Village. The compact house was a home to mill workers employed by the Roswell Manufacturing Company prior to and during the Civil War. It's situated in a beautiful area alongside other historic homes. Somewhere between these uses, however, the homes and their occupants failed to flourish. When I first started renting an office in the area almost twenty years ago, every building was run down. Where there was once a lush city park, an overgrown dump was sprawled in the center of the village. Homes were in various stages of disrepair, many boarded up with plywood.

But when I stood before the dilapidated home that would become my office, I saw its potential. The two front doors of the duplex were still there. Behind the 1970s paneling, the old 1-by-6 planks still stood. Under the Sheetrock ceiling, I discovered old post and beam construction with wood pegs instead of nails. And tearing away thick, dirty shag carpeting revealed heart pine flooring.

The ability to be able to help others find their life's work, in the center of a village that had been built on work, was birthed from an inkling I first had fifteen years ago. Although I didn't have the money at the time to renovate, I knew I wanted to work in an environment where I'd sit on my front porch and share life with my neighbors and my clients. After visiting my banker, Frank, about a loan to purchase the property, he phoned my consulting clients to ask them what kind of guy I was. And when Frank reached out to the clients into whom I'd poured my life and energy, relationship equity magically morphed into financial equity.

Once I had a commitment from the bank, Dave, a good friend, believed in me and my vision and loaned me $5,000. So though the building eventually took money, getting started didn't. Getting started required vision and action. Without enough money to buy the house, it required making and keeping an appointment with Frank and asking Dave to spot me the cash.

As the Beatles crooned, "I get by with a little help from my friends." Part of using what you have as you pursue your life's work is noticing who may be able to help. In my case, the confidence of my consulting clients was enough for Frank to loan me the money. Sometimes we fail to recognize that the community we already have can help us do what we need to do.

As you consider your own calling, close your eyes and notice the faces of the folks who already share your life. They might be family or friends or neighbors or colleagues or elders from your church. Maybe one of them is financially savvy. Perhaps one of them has a flair for design and color. One might be a "big picture" visionary and another might be more attentive to "micro details." There may even be someone in this gallery of characters who'd be willing to harness a diverse team to guide and support you as you step into your calling.

Having More Than Meets the Eye

A few years back I realized that almost every trip I was making to Rwanda was so crammed with appointments, meetings, and conferences—the stuff of entrepreneurship—that the "social" part of being a social entrepreneur had suffered. So, during one visit, I purposed to spend a bit of extra time with our staff at the Ruli Mountain coffee washing station.

One afternoon I joined our team sitting in a circle under the site's broad canopy. As we surveyed our pulping machine, fermentation tanks, and drying tables, I also wanted us to share what was at work in our hearts.

Gloriose, a tall and stunning woman, is our director of production; Alex is our thoughtful, deliberate, focused wash station manager; Geraldine is our petite, attentive accountant; Aimee is our young, energetic director of fermentation. One by one, each person shared their story.

Aimee, who was orphaned by the genocide when he was a teenager, revealed that he had no mother, no father, no brothers, and no sisters. Our country director, Manny, had told me that Aimee had been found sleeping at our washing station. I'd asked Manny to offer him a job, and Aimee soon became a critical part of our team as the director of fermentation at Bukonya.

Tragically, when Aimee pursued a trial with the local tribunal to reclaim his family's land from the "genocidaires" who'd murdered his family, the leaders ruled against him. From the moment of their verdict, Aimee had wanted to leave Bukonya. So when we purchased the Ruli Mountain washing station in a nearby region, Manny invited Aimee to leave Bukonya and join us in Ruli for a fresh start.

At the end of each day, Rwandans sit around the fire and enjoy time together as a community to share the highs and the lows of the day. This time is traditionally called *igitaromo*. As we gathered in this circle, Aimee shared that he considered Land of a Thousand Hills to be family. He'd come to think of me as his father and his co-workers as brothers and sisters. Though he was once alone, Aimee explained, he now had coffee, co-workers, and me.

Gloriose shared that she knew Aimee was wanting to build his own house and eventually be married. In Rwandan culture, if a man cannot afford his own home, he cannot take on the responsibility of marriage. Gloriose revealed that she and Alex and Geraldine had all been saving their money to buy sand and mortar for Aimee's eventual house. Manny Gatare had agreed to buy the doors and windows. Then, tentatively, Gloriose asked if I'd consider buying the bricks. After witnessing the family love between these co-workers—no, among these brothers and sisters—I was delighted to be included. Not long after my contribution, St. Peter's Place, the congregation I serve in Georgia, agreed to purchase the roof. In time, many others caught the vision and joined in to build Aimee's house.

Aimee had a desire to build a house.

He shared his desire with his friends.

His friends shared both his desire and their commitment with me.

Seeing Aimee's desire and the team's commitment, I shared both with my church.

A house was built.

The relationships you have now are the relationships you will need to live out your calling. Have you shared your desire with others? Scrappers who are dogged about responding to

God's call are those willing to launch with the tools, training, money, and relationships they already have.

How to *Scrap*

As you consider the breadth of resources at your disposal, keep a notebook close to your bed or workstation so you can jot these down as they occur to you. As you begin to catalog these, you may discover you have more to work with than you'd imagined. In this notebook you can gather contact information for the friends of friends who might lend you a pricey tool or scribble down the website where you can learn more about scholarships for the training you need. You can note which of your parents' friends might be able to introduce you to the next right person who's doing something similar to your dream. Or you can remind yourself to connect with the friend from high school who's thriving in Hollywood. If you're willing to be creative and a little scrappy, this notebook will become a treasure map pointing you to a wealth of available resources.

I've always been a bit of a scrapper myself. When I was thirteen, my dad bought me my first car: a burgundy 1971 MGB. The MG was well rusted by the Indiana road salt, but she was mine. Two years before I'd even have my driver's license, I began sanding the rust off. Then Dad welded on a piece of galvanized steel that would function as the fender, and I proceeded to sculpt the new fender with Bondo adhesive. When the car was finished, the fender was so heavy that the whole vehicle listed to one side. The MG was the first of dozens of fixer-uppers I've refurbished over the years.

During my freshman year at Cedarville College, I salvaged old wood from an abandoned lumber mill to maximize our tiny space by building a loft. My use-what-you-have mentality continued after graduation when I worked alongside a few plumbers laying the pipework at the Georgia Terrace Hotel across from the historic Fox Theater. I had two master's degrees, but as a recent grad, I needed money. As I was digging ditches, I knew there was more in my future: one day I would build lives.

In 2006, when I had the first inkling to start Land of a Thousand Hills, I had to use what I had as well. I'd been married twelve years and had established a successful coaching business. I met with several folks about the exciting possibility of forming a missional coffee business: Bishop John Rucyahana, my good Muslim friend Zia Khan, and a few Christian friends from church. After each meeting we'd each have tasks we'd agreed to accomplish. I was surprised to discover that few from the US, with the exception of my friend Zia, followed through. One business-minded friend said he'd investigated possibilities, but he was unable to find a way to export the coffee. Others had agreed that they thought it was a good idea but took no action to move forward. Concerned that pursuing the call "by committee" wouldn't be fruitful, my wife and I decided that we'd move forward as a family, working in a way that drew our family together rather than working through the church or a nonprofit.

As I glance back at the beginnings of Land of a Thousand Hills, it's clear I didn't have anything that approximated the right tools, training, money, or relationships to launch a coffee business. But as I began, I discovered that when I decided to be who God had created and redeemed me to be, I was able to respond to God's calling using what I had.

As you're reading this, I wonder if perhaps you already have the resources you need to get started on your calling. What tools do you have to use right now? What training might be trans-ferrable to your new inkling? Genius, I am told, is harnessing the discipline of one field of study and applying it to another. How can you use the little money you have to creep toward your new endeavor? What about your relationships? Once you have a passion for something, others will catch your fire and get involved. Believe it or not, the people in your life right now are most likely the community God will use to help your vision become a reality.

1. Have you ever hesitated to jump in feet first because you didn't think you had what you needed?
2. Have you ever had a moment when you took a leap of faith using only what you had?
3. Right now, what is one "next step" you could take?

– 4 –

Four Hundred Years
of Coffee

Get What You Can

When my brother Tim and I were children, imagination was the sparked flint that fueled our days.

We'd fly through the back door with the screen door swinging behind us, jump off the second step past the sandbox, and soar out the back gate. Passing through the field of vertical crosses marking our dearly departed pets, we'd hang a right and run up the wooded neighborhood trail, careful to avoid slipping into holes that might have traps in them.

I'm proud to note that these traps weren't left behind by suburban hunters; these grand inventions were all mine. I'd dig a hole and fill it with ammo: old peanut butter and jelly sandwiches, tin cans, thorn bushes, and anything else I'd rustle up.

I'd carefully cover the opening with thin branches, leaves, and a bit of sand. When an unsuspecting friend or enemy would step on it—BINGO!

Dashing past the traps, we'd cross over a deep ditch on the bridge we'd made to reach our fort. Built around four trees, it was three stories high.

I don't think we ever bought a piece of wood for that sky-scraper. We did ask Dad for scraps from his home improvement projects. We dragged home plywood from what others had left on the curb to be hauled away. Once we even went to the construction site on Hamstrom Road to ask the builder for some of the wood in his inventory.

The only money we ever spent on our fort was for nails from the hardware store. The world I knew expanded exponentially the day Mom let me walk with Tim to Portage Hardware. I clutched a handful of loose change the whole way.

Bud and his sister lived on one side of the building and ran the hardware store out of the other. If we needed something when they were closed, Bud instructed us to take a quarter and knock on the door. When the storefront side was locked up, I dropped most of my change into my small pocket and held a quarter in my fist. I proceeded to knock with my knuckles, unsure how it was making a difference. After a few minutes I realized I was supposed to tap the glass door with the quarter. (This made so much more sense.) Bud steered his wheelchair to the door, unlocked it, and asked what we needed.

"I'd like to buy sixteen penny nails, please, Mr. Bud," I said.

When Bud handed us the sack, we dashed home to start building the next phase of our fort.

Learning to ask and get what you can is as crucial in building a life, and in pursuing a calling, as it is in building forts.

A Few Clever Scrappers

Kevin is a friend of a friend. During the three years Kevin was in divinity school, he dreamed of a ministry to young men leaving the juvenile justice system—not everyone's dream! Upon graduation, he wanted to open a home where these guys could transition back into society, learning how to function and thrive in a healthier environment than the one that had shaped them. From the outside, nothing Kevin brought to the table would have indicated that he'd been called to this mighty work. He didn't bring money, experience, or the wisdom that comes with age. In fact, he was only twenty-five years old!

The slim résumé didn't dissuade Kevin.

He began by roping in a dream team advisory board. The leaders he chose were wise, experienced, and passionate. One of these was a well-connected man with a lot of local contacts. As Kevin was searching for property for his venture, this leader tapped a wealthy associate who agreed to purchase the house where this transformational community would take root.

Kevin lived into his calling by getting what he could.

I used to advise my coaching clients that if they weren't happy where they were, they could move. I instructed, "You can move. You are not a tree."

In Genesis 12, God commanded Abraham to get up and leave his homeland.

Abraham wondered, "Where?"

God explained, "To the place I will show you."

"Yeah," Abraham had to be thinking, "but . . . actually . . . where?"

Abraham took that first step of his journey without knowing the destination.

One of my heroes on this planet is a young man named Manu—a popular name in Rwanda. Five years ago, I was visiting the rural parish of Kiryamo with Karen, one of our team members, when I caught a glimpse of young Manu, who was about fourteen years old, dragging himself down the dirt road by the church. Placing both hands on the ground, he'd lift his rear up off the ground and slide a few inches. Then he'd do the same thing again, creeping forward. When I asked the church rector about him, he explained that Manu was paralyzed. I'd never known or seen anyone who was paralyzed function without a wheelchair, and Karen arranged for Manu to receive a wheelchair.

When I visited a year later, young Manu was navigating his wheelchair through the area's dirt roads and steep terrain like a master. Manu has a face that glows with joy and mighty arms like oak limbs.

Three years after that, Manu went to chat in confidence with our collaborative trade director, Manny Gatare. Explaining to Manny that he had no feeling below his waist, he asked in desperation if he'd ever be a man.

After noodling on the question a moment, Manny affirmed, "Well, you are."

Tears leaking down his smooth brown cheeks, Manu protested, "I cannot walk, and I have no feeling. Will I ever function as a man?"

Manny put his arms on Manu's shoulders and offered, "We can pray, and we will act."

After they prayed and Manu left the office, Manny called me to ask if we could find funds to take Manu to Kigali to visit a specialist. When they finally made the journey, the neurosurgeons told them nothing could be done. When Manny shared the disappointing news with me, I grieved.

Six months later, I had occasion to visit Kiryamo again. Singing and dancing children greeted me as is typical. As the celebration wound down, I noticed a man using crude forearm crutches.

One slow step after the next, young Manu—towering at more than six feet—walked toward me. He shook my hand and gave me a hug. Manu explained that he'd asked his community to help and to pray. Then he used what he had—his strong arms—to move toward his dream. Tears fell from my eyes. I was shocked to learn that he'd had no medical intervention: only prayer and determination.

Your calling may not demand an advisory board or a neurosurgeon. Getting what you need might spring from something as simple as a dozen donuts.

Twelve Delicious Reasons to Help Us and One Good "Ask"

When I worked with the pipe fitters one summer, my dad encouraged me to take donuts to the millwrights who worked for Bethlehem Steel. I wasn't entirely sure why Dad had me do this, but every Monday when I'd walk in with a dozen donuts they'd smile and thank me and we'd share a joke. They didn't make a lot of money, but they had big responsibility and a lot of equipment at their disposal.

A few months later, the day came when we needed a "cherry picker," a large industrial crane, to move a massive piece of pipe. Cherry pickers cost about five thousand dollars a day to rent, and we only needed one for a few hours.

Dad instructed me, "Jon, go see the millwrights you've been taking donuts to. They've got a cherry picker."

Though it seemed like a big ask, they were happy to help. The foreman assured me, "I'll have Joe right over to do the work for you."

A few dozen donuts, a smile, and a laugh saved us five thousand dollars.

As you consider getting what you can in the pursuit of your calling, it's wise to invest in relationships.

Sometimes these relationships will yield measurable benefits to you, and other times you may need to take a risk by asking for what you need. If you're serving in overseas missions, you might ask a circle of supporters for financial assistance. If you're building a business, you might ask a businessman at church to serve as your mentor. If you're starting to work from home, you might need to ask an elderly neighbor to sit in your living room during the kids' naptime so you can run to the post office. The worst that can happen when you ask for what you need is that you'll get a no and move on. The best that can happen is that you'll be one baby step closer to your calling.

My friend Eric is a postulant to become an ordained deacon in our church. He shared with me that he wanted to take a ninety-day, eight-hours-a-day class for app developers. While that sounds like a great plan for someone who might be adrift, Eric had just finished his master of divinity at a prestigious seminary. His life was full too: he worked full-time for his dad, served as my right-hand man at church, and was recently married. So I was a bit hesitant to jump on board the app train too quickly.

But I can get behind Eric because I know that his vision for ministry is dual-vocational: with one foot in the church and one in the marketplace. Though he did it with fear and trembling,

Eric asked his dad if he'd invest in him, underwriting part of the cost of the course. Generously, his dad agreed. Today Eric is developing an app for his dad's company and has three other contracts waiting.

Eric took a risk and asked.

The path to our callings often challenges us to get what we can. As you trace the contours of the journey toward your calling that's brought you this far, you may notice those points at which you've already gotten what you could. Maybe you entered and won a contest which gave you a remarkable opportunity. Perhaps you met somebody along the path who's continued to journey beside you. Maybe your hard work on the job was rewarded with a promotion. As I glance back over my shoulder, I can recognize a number of points at which I got what I could.

The Unusual Journey to Getting What I Could

Kneeling on a red-velvet-covered kneeling bench, I bowed my head and closed my eyes as five sets of hands came to rest on my back and shoulders. I was being ordained into the Anglican Communion, a gathering of eighty million Christians worldwide in thirty-nine provinces.

My inkling to plant a church had led me to this moment and specifically to the Rwandan branch of the Communion. As an Anglican, I was now part of a worldwide community working together in harmony.

Rwandan Bishop John Rucyahana had been part of that crew who'd ordained me. And when he explained to me that prior to the genocide his country had grown good coffee and that it had been their greatest national export, I'd rallied the folks I thought could contribute. But when the response was halfhearted, I didn't give up.

After researching for countless hours on the internet, I discovered that Michigan State and Texas A&M had already been working with Rwandan coffee growers through a USAID project. I contacted my friend Ann, who referred me to a man named Tim Schilling in Rwanda. Tim was an agronomist from Texas A&M University who had invested his skill and life in post-genocide Rwanda. My friend Zia, a gifted graphic design artist, spent many hours developing our brand using the tools and training he had, alongside the money and relationships I shared.

This is how Land of a Thousand Hills began.

When I shared my vision with Tim, he liked it, referring me to Alan Odum from InterAmerican Coffee. Alan had taken the big risk of ordering an entire container of coffee from the Gashonga cooperative: 320 sacks. I decided that I would purchase 20 of those bags, or 2,600 pounds of coffee. I was willing to take the risk. What was the worst that could happen? I'd own a 400-year supply of coffee, and my friends and family would receive it as gifts for years!

It took almost eight months for the coffee to arrive. During that time I purchased a used twelve-pound roaster off of eBay. (So now I had a roaster to pay for on top of the twenty sacks of coffee!) I visited my banker friend Frank, who'd loaned me the money for my office, and shared the Land of a Thousand Hills vision with him. Graciously, Frank agreed to the bank loaning the start-up capital.

I consulted with a monk from the Monastery of the Holy Spirit who was engaged in a similar work in South America.

When my roaster arrived, the craftsman who built it, a guy named Dion, talked me through rewiring it.

When the coffee arrived, Dion referred me to a well-known coffee consultant who spent four days teaching me to roast and cup coffee.

I began contacting the eighty Anglican churches who already had an affinity for Rwanda, delighted to find there was interest. But I also realized that I didn't have the time or interest to become a full-time salesperson.

One spring afternoon I was roasting in my first-floor office when Robert Crow, the English guy who rented a second-floor office from me, came barreling down the stairs in a fluster because he thought the office was on fire!

Nope, I explained—just roasting coffee.

Though I'd invited Robert to church a number of times, he'd always chuckled and declined attending religious services with the landlord. But when he saw me roasting coffee, Rob became intrigued. When I shared with him the Rwandan story, he became interested in learning more. We scheduled an evening at a local pub called The Harp to enjoy a pint together. As we each tossed back a Guinness, Rob and I became friends. In fact, he even announced that he wanted to leave his position in educational sales in order to come work with me.

I can say, in good conscience, that I tried to talk him out of it: I informed him that the pay was lower, it was a risk, and he'd be selling to churches. I could not, however, dissuade him. And am I ever glad for that, as Rob was so instrumental to our growth. But Land of a Thousand Hills was also instrumental in his growth: two years later, Rob became a follower of God.

Two thousand six hundred pounds of coffee.

One twelve-pound roaster.

One twenty-thousand-dollar loan.

One curious and talented tenant.

As I responded to God's calling, I got what I could.

Just as every person's journey toward their calling is different, getting what you can looks different as well. Sometimes you'll scour the web and finally find what you need on eBay. Or you'll ask a friend of a friend to introduce you to the person who can help you take your next brave step. You might gather your courage, don your best suit, and ask a local banker for a loan.

Getting what you can isn't about you at all. It's about you taking the next faithful step in the direction the One who's calling you is leading.

1. Have you ever invested in a relationship—not expecting anything in return—that turned out to be useful later on?

2. Is there a person in your life today who might help you take the next step in your journey?

3. Right now, what is one "next step" you could take?

– 5 –

When Life Says, "Come Hither"

Follow the Inkling

The wave of dissatisfaction wasn't what I'd expected at the conclusion of a successful consulting project.

The vice president of finance for a large insurance company had invited me to work with the entire finance staff in order to lead them through my Lifeswork process to help each one identify their calling in life and, ideally, integrate it into their role within the company. I'd embraced the job of leading forty men and women through the process as a welcome adventure. The work we'd done together had been successful. Some of the participants discovered that they were doing exactly what they were made to do. These were on the road to even greater productivity. Others identified and pursued other more satisfying roles within the walls of the corporate headquarters.

One woman who'd thought for a while about becoming a teacher was affirmed that teaching was indeed her natural gifting. She transferred to the training department and embraced new work that mattered to her and to the company. Other employees chose to leave their jobs and did so with the blessing of their supervisors. The staff told me they felt cared for throughout the process.

So why was I feeling unsettled? Well, the process with this corporate team had opened a window to reflect on the work that I was called to do.

I said before that I didn't know too many pastors whose lives I wanted to emulate. For the most part, the male pastors I knew seemed to fall into three camps.

Some were focused and determined but communicated a self-righteous arrogance. They lived with a conviction that they were always in the know and always right. They struck me as the equivalent of Christian mercenaries: grasping, greedy, claiming a self-proclaimed monopoly on the truth.

Others were more meek but seemed like "kept men." They were tender and gentle. The kind of people you go to for counsel and comfort if you have a problem. But they lacked passion, any fire in their belly. Rather than embracing the adventure of living as God's person, they more often seemed "corralled" by leadership teams of their congregations.

The third group of pastors were my kind of people. These were women and men willing to embrace the mystery of the holy. They were willing to risk reputation to fight for what they believed in. I admired their honesty and determination. But I wasn't sure if it was for me.

My friend Ron, who'd been my youth pastor years earlier, had love in his heart and fire in his belly, and he lived a passionate life of faithfulness to God and service to others. And yet because his church had always considered him a renegade, they often thwarted his call rather than supported it.

Despite the grim prospects about what it looked like to move into full-time ministry, I'd still entertain the idea now and then. And I wasn't alone. For years, my friends and family had wondered if I'd become a pastor.

Not surprisingly, during that season, I had a pastor who was bold and aggressive and full of life. As I shared the possibility of pastoring with him, Warren turned toward me, locked his gaze to mine, and demanded, "You need to do your business or get off the pot. You have the means and the gifts."

His eloquent words still rang in my ears when I was summoned to meet with the vice president of human resources at the insurance company. The vice president of finance had made a move to another company, and just a day earlier I'd opened the mailbox at my office to find my final check for the work I'd done. When I met with the HR exec, he thanked me for my work and curtly let me know that they'd no longer be implementing my program.

I'd just invested a year of my life into this project and these people. As a result, the employees reported being more fulfilled in their work. And though the fellow who'd hired me had counted it a roaring success, now, because of internal politics, I stood at the edge of a vast corporate ocean and watched helplessly as a significant investment of my life's work was washed away. Had the energy and passion and effort I'd poured into these folks been futile?

Reenter the chronic inkling.

What would it be like, I mused, to pastor a church? In lieu of receiving the proverbial "pink slip" at the whim of others, severing the relationships I'd been building, what would be different about pouring my life into a small group of people through births and baptisms, marriages and anniversaries, illness and death?

A few days after I'd been "released" from working with that company, Brenda and I traveled to Indiana to spend Christmas with my family. One of the highlights for me was spending time with my nephew the day after we'd arrived. We spent most of the afternoon hiking and discussing a relationship in his life with which he was struggling.

That evening before dinner, on the heels of this great conversation with my nephew, I sprawled on the double bed in the guest room and stared at the ceiling, asking myself, "What have I been doing for ten years?"

I knew I was a good consultant.

The decade had been financially lucrative.

But what I really loved, my nephew had reminded me, was people and not business.

I at last gave myself permission to dwell in the cloud of vaporous possibility that had been hovering over me for years. To breathe it in. To let it wash over me. To the sound of the tick-tock alarm clock beside the bed, I toyed with the idea of planting a church. As Brenda lay beside me later that evening, I took the risk of mentioning it.

"That seems about right," she replied.

When we returned home to Atlanta and I floated it past get-off-the-pot Warren, he invited me to help plant a church.

God's Gracious Pub Provision

A few weeks later, when I dropped into The Harp Irish Pub with my friend Greg, we caught the end of a set by a talented guitarist. Greg himself was a great songwriter and guitar player. I asked him what he thought about playing music in a church. Though surprised by the suggestion, he considered it for a few days and agreed.

Then I did what I coached my clients to do. I talked with folks who were doing what I was considering. Specifically, I asked three other people about the texture of their lives in pastoral or parachurch ministry. In the first conversation, one pastor said that he could envision me in a pastoral role as I continued to consult. Another gave me the tired old advice, "Only do it if it's the only thing you can do."[4] The third came alive as he described the joy he experienced walking with people through the journeys of their lives.

The inkling to plant a church and pastor a congregation was like the soapy bubble of an idea that had drifted past my purview so many times throughout my life. Until now I'd noticed it and mused, "Hmm . . . well, that's interesting," as I watched it float by. Finally, though, I stuck out a finger and popped it.

Thirteen years later, I am still the rector at St. Peter's Place. In fact, it has become one of the defining investments of my life.

I'm not convinced that God has a specific will for our lives. I don't know that there's one "right plan" or that we're at grave risk of missing out the way we'd miss a train if we arrived at the station five minutes after it departed. I am sure that God has whimsy. In his book *Love Does*, my friend Bob Goff explains, "Whimsy doesn't care if you are the driver or the passenger; all that matters is that you are on your way."[5] I see God engaging with each one of us as we're on the way.

God creates new ventures and initiatives and invites us to join him. God is at work and invites us into the adventure. If we choose not to respond to God's invitation, the world doesn't end. The next speeding train that barrels by doesn't smash us for our "disobedience." We just miss out. And when the next train does slow down near the platform, we have another opportunity to hop on board.

Running with my inkling was a matter of noticing what occupied my thoughts. I realized I'd been imagining what it would be like to pastor a brave, faithful congregation of believers who were committed to God and to each other. I know one woman who discovered her inkling by trusting others. Members of her church recognized her gifts and saw what she might become. Willing to take one brave step, she signed up for some classes that confirmed what they'd noticed about her unique gifts. Perhaps your inkling has been percolating since childhood. You may have swatted it aside or reasoned it away, but the possibility birthed years ago still bubbles inside. Maybe your inkling is the answer to the question, "If money were no object, and you could be anything in the world, what would you be?" There are a host of ways you might stumble upon your inkling. Begin to notice those percolating possibilities that enliven you.

"Come Along, and Let's See How This Goes"

During one of my early trips to Bukonya, Rwanda, where we built our first coffee washing station, the children from a local orphanage wrote a song and choreographed a dance that they performed during a worship service. Twenty children under the age of ten, all dressed in white, erupted into joyful singing, drumming, and dancing. Some dipped low to the ground, imitating traditional Rwandan dance. Others stretched to the sky as they waved their hands in praise.

Though I'm not much of a dancer, I do know how to dance the Israeli folk dance called the Hava Nagila, which means "let us rejoice." It was composed in the 1920s and has become a staple at Jewish weddings and ceremonies. The bouncy children continued singing and dancing in a circle and I, with my rear near the ground, kicked my legs out in front of me with my arms folded across my chest. When it was time to continue the service and I was winded, I asked my friend Ildephonse to interpret the meaning of the children's lyrics.

He explained, "Satan had his eyes on us to destroy us, but God invited you, American, to help save us."

What a theology! God was indeed intent on saving those orphans. I think he would have done it with or without me, but he invited me to join in on what he was up to. God was on a dangerous adventure and wanted me to be part of it.

This is the way God works. He doesn't demand that we do something but rather says, "Come along, and let's see how this goes." If we choose not to respond or we don't recognize God's voice, God doesn't become enraged with us. No, God carries on with the adventure, and when another comes along for which we're well suited, he invites again. The myth that you've been made for one thing—and that you're at grave risk of missing out on that one thing—isn't found in the pages of God's book. Rather, God's Spirit offers countless entry points to the adventure you were made to live.

In coaching others to find their life's work, I've encountered many people who've told me that they've wanted to find God's will for their lives. In fact, after her third coaching session, one woman demanded that I tell her God's will for her life. I answered, "You aren't paying me enough for that!"

She viewed God's will as something static that would be mysteriously discovered or mystically imparted. She saw God's will as an external directive to discover and perform rather than an internal impulse for which she was created and through which she would most naturally co-create with God.

I am not sure that God calls us from the future as much as he creates us from the past and the present.

Created and Called

The author of Psalm 139 assures us that God created us in our mothers' wombs, that we've been crafted intentionally in intricate detail. I also believe that God created us each with specific talents and gifts. When those talents and gifts combine with our life's experience, they're appropriated in service to the world.

In the twentieth chapter of Exodus, the Israelites had just been delivered from slavery. They were learning to trust God, and God delivered to them, through Moses, the Ten Commandments.

He told them, "I am the Lord your God who brought you out of slavery. So don't bow to any of those old Gods of productivity and work and production that ruled in Egypt."

"Don't make for yourself a graven image because that's not God. I am."

"Each week, take a day of rest because I am the God of rest."

God continued to school this recently liberated community on how free people should treat each other. Then Moses climbed the mountain and received further detailed instructions about how to build the temple. While Moses was on his business trip, the Hebrew people proceeded to break most of the commandments.

In the message Moses delivered, though, is this interesting bit about a guy named Bezalel:

See, I have chosen Bezalel son of Uri, the son of Hur, of the tribe of Judah, and I have filled him with the Spirit of God, with wisdom, with understanding, with knowledge and with all kinds of skills—to make artistic designs for work in gold, silver and bronze, to cut and set stones, to work in wood, and to engage in all kinds of crafts. (Exod. 31:1–5 NIV)

God had sculpted Bezalel, in his mom's womb, to be creative. And God was inviting him to use that skill to build the temple. Bezalel was no longer enslaved; he had free will to accept or decline the prospective gig. Part of following an inkling—even the kinds that don't come with explicit instructions from the lips of the Almighty—is attending to that voice inviting you to be who you are by using the gifts you've been given.

We often ask questions of God like, "What is your will for my life?" and "What do you want me to do?" And yet these rigid questions fail to honor the God who is living and active and walking beside us on the journey. God has created us to serve him using the skills and interests and longings and passions we've been given. God doesn't design robots; God designs children who learn and grow and develop over a lifetime.

Perhaps instead we should be asking questions of God that are more attuned to our lives and stories, like:

- How have you created me?
- What are the experiences which have formed me?
- What gifts do I have to offer this world?
- How can I serve the common good?

Then wait.
Notice the faint whisper of an inkling.

Take one brave step.

Psychologist Abraham Maslow has suggested that finding your vocation is like finding a mate. You date your work, and your work dates you. If it's not a love connection, the second date probably won't happen. But if you have a good first date, you want a second. There's a mutual vetting process.

Jeff's Brave Step

My friend Jeff is a single dad, divorced, and a recovering alcoholic. One of the things I most love about Jeff is that he is also an avid implementer of inklings. A few years back he attended a men's retreat where he was invited to consider his call. The inkling that Jeff had been toying with was sort of a vague possibility of helping guys be guys.

Jeff had heard an interesting story about buffalo, of all things, that had sort of stuck in his craw. When buffalo are faced with an impending storm, they huddle up and charge the storm. Specifically, the vulnerable beasts—typically the young and the old—are sheltered at the center of the herd. Though the instinct and behavior of cows is to scatter and run alone from a storm, buffalo weather danger together. And while the cows tire and are overtaken by the storm, buffalo are on the other side much more quickly.

Inkling = buffalo.

Jeff knew he wanted to do something with the buffalo.

He coined the name Legacy Builders and hired a designer to sketch a buffalo head logo, with the goal of launching a movement of dads investing in their sons. When I first met Jeff, he held a buffalo head nickel between his thumb and forefinger and told me the story of the buffalo and cows. He ended with,

"You are a buffalo, and as a result of being a buffalo, you have become a chief." When I gave one of these nickels with a buffalo on one side and a Native American chief on the other to my dad, I showed him the buffalo and said, "Dad, you've done what buffalo do: face the storm to protect their young. You're still doing it." Then I turned it over and explained, "After years of being a buffalo, you become a chief."

Jeff living into his calling affirmed my dad in his.

When inklings are given attention, fed, and watered, they can grow into beautiful expressions of vocation.

Inklings Can Be Signaled by Play

In her book *Mindfulness*, Ellen Langer claims that the chief objective in life is to blur the lines between work and play. So if you're not able to play, you will likely not perceive an inkling.

Have you ever paused to watch a child play in his or her own world of wonder? Maybe he's organizing books on shelves to build a "library." Or pushing a bulldozer through a sandbox. Maybe she's taping boxes together to create a condominium for plastic action figures. Or creating a new game by kicking a rubber playground ball against the side of the house. In children's play, an inkling often unfolds and is implemented. Within safe boundaries, a child at play is free of constricting rules, roles, and responsibilities. (Playing in chaos is difficult.)

What would it look like for you to create a structure in which you allowed yourself to play? Perhaps you'd borrow a bucket of Legos from the kid down the street and design your dream kitchen. Or maybe you'd set up a palette of paints beside an easel with a blank canvas without a plan for what to paint. Maybe you'd jump in a lake, float on your back, and notice what ideas drifted in and out of your mind. Or maybe you'd strap on a pair of rented roller skates and start skating. Purposing to play is one way to release the possibilities that have been shelved or sidelined or squashed over the years.

I suspect that play was part of God's good intention for Sabbath rest in Genesis. After six days of work, God instructed, rest. During that day you're not working, even if for a few hours, make space to play. Leave your iPhone on your desk. Let people know you'll be out of touch and do something you enjoy. My favorite go-to play during my rest time is to take a long walk in the woods with my dogs where both my mind and my body can wander unfettered. I'm not as disciplined as I'd like to be about taking a full day of Sabbath each week, but when I do I am recharged and ready to recognize the next inkling that I'm beginning to notice in the periphery of my experience.

The challenge with apprehending what's on the periphery is that you're more often focused on the task or goal at hand. When you have no margins or opportunity to notice what's on the outskirts, you won't.

If you're committed to become more aware of these inklings, one strategy is to leave unscheduled blocks of time in your day. As you build in margin, you'll be more likely to notice inklings on the margins. Or, on your next vacation, schedule time just to wander and discover.

The Tenth Man

A story I read recently describes a Jewish man on his way to the temple for his holy days. He had to arrive there before sundown on the Friday before the Sabbath. As he rushed to meet his rabbi, he stopped in a small village for a drink of water. While he was there, a man pleaded with him to stay and pray. They had nine men and needed a tenth to form the minyan, a group of ten Jewish men requisite to form a public worship and thus be considered a congregation.

At their invitation, the man protested that he had to leave to meet his rabbi.

They begged, "Please, we cannot pray without you."

Again, he refused.

A final time they pleaded for him to pray with them. And yet, dutiful to meet his rabbi, he rushed off to the adjacent village, arriving at the synagogue just before sundown.

"Rabbi," he panted, out of breath, "I am struggling to follow God's call. After I finished my work for the day, I ran as fast as I could to get here, even avoiding staying to help nine faithful men in the next village who were begging me to pray with them. Now I am here. Please speak to me on behalf of the Lord."

Stroking his beard, the rabbi replied, "My son, you remember those nine men? Today you were to be the tenth man!"

The man's intent focus on what was before him kept him from recognizing the opportunity to respond to God's call right beside him. It's no mistake that the physical design of our bodies, when they're functioning as they were created to do, is to receive optical information from the edges of our vision as well as the center.

Implicit in the definition of an "inkling" is acting on it before you are certain. If your hunch is an obvious certainty, it's not an inkling.

What about that inkling that's been squatting in your periphery for a good while now? Name it, write it down, and share it with someone close to you. Devote some time, invest some resources, create some space to make a little wiggle room where you can determine whether your inkling will take root or wither away.

Toying with Our Inklings

Recently I've been considering the idea of being a shepherd. I don't mean "pastor" shepherd; I mean keeper of actual, wooly, four-legged sheep. Though I can't pinpoint the exact reason, something continues to draw me to it. I'm familiar with the many biblical stories involving sheep, and I see how God has used them to communicate timeless truths. Curious, I poked around the web to learn more. I learned that not only do these marvelous creatures produce wool for clothing, they also offer milk that's high in nutrition, their waste is "pelletized" so it makes less of a stinky mess, and their meat is known to be quite tasty.

What have I done about this unlikely inkling?

I started with the research. Then I shared the inkling with my wife, who chuckled lovingly. I spoke to Diana Wiley of True Vineyard Ministries. True Vineyard keeps sheep in Rwanda as a way of serving widows who create yarn. And now my friend and country director Manny Gatare is looking for potential sheep land. I don't know where this is headed, but I'm taking one step at a time.

Although my friend Bob Pattillo was financially successful in real estate, he recognized that he still wasn't satisfied. So he pursued a trip to Bangladesh to explore the possibility of investing there.

On Bob's trip he met a petite Bangladeshi woman who was a microentrepreneur. When Bob asked her what her dream in life was, she told him that it was to walk down the street with her husband, head held high, knowing that she was caring for her family financially.

She then turned to Bob and asked with dignity, "What are your dreams?"

Today, Bob names that moment as a turning point for him. He realized that the power of the microloan is that the borrower sees herself as a client, not a charity case. She is a co-creator; the loan is a tool. At the same time she supplies the imagination, the true understanding of her community's needs and capabilities, and the grit. Bob has helped finance millions of microentrepreneurs and has launched over 1,400 schools for low-income kids in India.

Unlike so many successful business ventures, Bob's work didn't start with an exhaustive business plan. Rather, it began with an inkling and action.

The nature of experimenting with an inkling means that it won't necessarily lead anywhere. But that in itself is instructive! Inherent in toying with an inkling is possibility and risk and fun. It's considering the adventure that could be.

Not everyone is made like me. It may be that you are not wired to imagine extravagant possibilities. As you search for your calling, let the folks who know you best help you to see what might be in your blind spot. Ask a parent, "When I was five years old, what did you imagine I might become? What about when I was ten?" Or ask your college roommate, "When I was eighteen, what did you think my future might hold?" Or query a lifelong friend, "If there were no earthly limitations on what I might do or become, what do you see for me in your mind's eye?" Allow those who know and love you to reflect the possibilities that you might not yet see.

When my roommate and I were attending orientation at Rich-mont Graduate University, he pointed across the aisle toward Brenda and suggested, "There's one for you." When I noticed this spunky, confident girl wearing great-looking jeans and a green shirt, I was attracted to her. The first time I laid eyes on Brenda, the thought popped into my mind: "Hmm . . . I wonder what it would be like getting to know her?" It was an inkling. The inkling of attraction led to a two-year relationship in which we became best friends. Of course, most inklings don't pan out as well as they did for Brenda and me.

Divine Inklings

Sometimes I read the story of Abraham and wonder if his invita-tion from God wasn't more of an inkling than a command. In my mind's eye, I see him sitting in front of his tent looking at the stars and thinking about life, his family, his herds, and his work. Perhaps he was praying and thinking about what was to come.

And yet as this aged man prayed, I wonder if he didn't notice a hollowness, an emptiness. Did he have an inkling that change would be good, a sense he should get up and go, an urge to leave and engage the future?

I imagine everything in him filling with excitement. Did he have the spirit of a wanderer? Had he been feeling tied down and itchy for something more? Where would this inkling take him? Abraham responded with action to a voice that said, "I'll show you where." As Abraham took one step, and then the next, and the next, he fell into step with God, and they moved forward together.

As a Christian, I believe that I am in Christ, part of his mys-terious body and connected to him. I open my eyes to see where he might be communicating with me already. Central to that communication is word, written and spoken. While some pagan religions center on visions and pictures, the Judeo-Christian tradition pays close attention to word. In the beginning, God spoke creation into existence with a word.

One way to feast on God's Word that many have found helpful is called *Lectio Divina*, which means "divine reading." This practice makes space to noodle on inklings. You read a portion of Scripture and meditate on it. You don't focus on the exegesis or the doctrine but rather just read and let the story settle in. You might ask:

> *In this story, who do I relate to?*
> *If I were one of these characters, who would I be?*
> *Would I have responded like that guy did?*
> *What inklings come to mind?*

Another fruitful way to explore possibilities is to journal your own words. Give voice to your inner thoughts and feelings. As you do, the possibilities in your heart find voice. Then later, as you review your words, consider how you might be called to action.

I have a vision board I review often. It's a simple bulletin board where I will post pictures and words about what I'd like to achieve that are, as I'm tacking them up, inklings. The glossy magazine picture of a sheep is almost like a prayer that keeps this possibility before me.

A Few Six-Packs, One Friendly Rwandan, and an Amazon Blurb

The first time my coffee company, Land of a Thousand Hills, sold coffee at the Catalyst conference, we served 26,000 cups in three days. As the conference concluded, we loaded all of our gear into the truck, and the team drove it back to the warehouse to unload. On my way back, I swung by a grocery store to buy a couple of six-packs of beer to say thank you to my amazing team.

Walking from my car toward the automatic sliding entrance doors, I glanced up at the late afternoon sky and wondered, "God, what the flip am I doing?"

In casual conversation with the God who first called Abraham, I told God I was enjoying what I was doing. I felt like I'd given the coffee ministry some of my time, but if God was inviting me to give more I'd be willing. It didn't make sense: I have two master's degrees, I'm a pastor, and I'm an industrial psychologist. Why, I wondered, am I in coffee?

After grabbing the beer out of a cooler case, I stood in line to pay for it. When the woman who served me noticed the T-shirt I was wearing and I told her I worked with Rwandan coffee farms, she shared that she was from Nigeria.

Behind me I heard a feeble voice say, "Rwanda? I'm from Rwanda."

Turning around, I was faced with a dark-skinned woman in her early twenties. Her father had been an electrician in Rwanda and had wired the Sonrise School in Musanze where one of my adopted sons now attends. She shared that she'd just immigrated to the United States and was looking for an Anglican church. Surely, I mused, this couldn't have been a coincidence.

A few months later, on New Year's Day 2010, I went out for a run on our greenway in Roswell. A tree had fallen to the side of the path and stretched out into the lake. Pausing beside the tree, I peeked at the Facebook feed on my iPhone and noticed that another executive coach I know had written a book. The Amazon marketing promo referred to him as America's foremost coach.

The thought drifted through my mind, "I could be America's foremost coach."

It didn't make sense. I had a lot on my plate: pastoring at St. Peter's Place, consulting with CEOs, and providing Lifes-work coaching for private clients, plus I'd founded Land of a Thousand Hills four years earlier. Though most of my time was spent consulting, I was really enjoying the coffee business.

Stepping out onto the log over the lake, I stretched my hands up to God and asked, "What do you want me to do?"

Though I knew it wasn't the best question to be asking, it came out of my mouth anyway. Human nature, perhaps. At the time I had a tribe of seven coffee employees in the US and about five hundred farmers and a permanent staff person in Rwanda with whom I enjoyed working.

The same way Brenda had chuckled at my shepherd fantasy, I had a sense God was laughing. But this joyful laughter didn't have the "don't be ridiculous" tone to it. Instead, it rung with the freedom of, "What do you want to do? Look at your hands, look at your heart. What are you good at? What makes you come alive?"

The word that seemed to drift down from the heavens and land in my heart was *coffee.*

From a financial standpoint, it made no sense. In 2009, I'd billed $300,000 in consulting and coaching fees, allowing me to be my own bank for the coffee business. But in that six-letter word, I wanted to take another step.

And then another.

And then another.

Step by step, I continued to pursue what made me come alive.

Will you? Will you take one step and then another and then another as you pursue what makes you come alive?

It was an Amazon blurb that caused me to say, "I could be America's foremost coach," and then I decided to choose coffee. What has it been for you? Perhaps you've stood in front of a Georgia O'Keefe painting and mused, "I think I could do that." Or maybe you've heard stories from a friend who's a social worker and thought, "I think I'd like to do that." Or perhaps you've witnessed a friend launching a small enterprise out of her home and pondered whether you should start something too. When you honor those faint inklings of possibility, you're taking one more step into your calling.

1. What's that inkling that's been hanging in your periphery for a while now? Jot it down someplace and begin to explore it further.

2. If you asked significant people in your life what they imagined you becoming, what would they say? What did your parents see in you at age five? Or your roommate at age eighteen? What would a lifelong friend say he or she imagined you becoming?

3. Right now, what is one "next step" you could take?

– 6 –

Ashtrays and Ice Cream Cones

Pursue What Makes You Come Alive

Licking up chocolate drips running down the side of my ice cream cone, I noticed an elderly African American man cleaning each of the ashtrays in the outdoor arena. With a damp cloth he'd wipe each one until it shone silver again.

A confusing wave of sadness washed over me.

Why, I wondered, am I enjoying an ice cream cone while he is scrubbing ashtrays? Even at eight, I suspected that he was most likely working for close to nothing. As a child I had no tools to process either the complicated formula of economic social structures nor what an appropriate response might be. I didn't know if this man was satisfied with the work he'd been given. Perhaps he was even proud of his honest day's work.

I felt a strong urge to buy him an ice cream cone.

The moment was a formative one. As the years of my life unfolded, I'd have other opportunities to engage in relationship with those on the margins of a society. I'd eventually have a chance to buy and share meals with homeless men. To serve as a big brother to kids who didn't have dads during my college days. To deliver a turkey to Miss Donna, the widow down the street. To adopt ninety-year-old "Granny" up the street and take her to church. And eventually to work beside the people of Rwanda. God had knit into my heart a compassion for people.

Through the years I began to notice that I was able to help these folks on the margins—and as I did, I came alive.

When You Don't Enjoy Your People

A few years ago a member of my church started a ministry for women in the community around our church. Cassidy showed up at my office at 10:00 a.m. for the appointment we'd set to discuss the new venture.

"How's the ministry going?" I asked after we'd settled in.

"Well," she replied, "good."

I heard the words, but they didn't sound convincing.

She continued, "The women are being helped. They're learning about jobs, and I'm connecting them with community resources who can help them."

By outward appearances, she was doing everything right. But I still didn't recognize any spark of passion in Cassidy.

"Hmm," I mused. "Cassidy, you don't seem too excited."

"Well," she confessed, "really I'm not."

It was out.

"I . . . uh . . ." She stumbled as she searched for words. Finally, she admitted, "I don't like working with them."

Wanting to know more, I asked, "You mean there are difficult times?"

"No," she answered, with more strength now. "I don't like them."

I knew it had taken courage to admit.

"Then why are you working with them?" I asked, without any judgment in my voice. "If they're not your people, you'll never be effective with them. If you don't get excited about helping them, then you won't be with them long term."

Her anxious face seemed to soften with relief.

"Cassidy, if you don't really like working with these women, then stop. Jesus wants us to work with folks he's given us a heart for. Do you know why Jesus chose the disciples? Because he liked them. What's more, he loved them. They were his type of people. Rough and tumble scrappers."

I also added, "You see, if you are 'ministering' to people you don't really like, they'll feel it. And that doesn't work. People know if you are reaching out to them out of charity and duty."

Though I don't think she'd expected it, Cassidy left my office with a plan both to tap new leadership for the ministry and also to notice who she did enjoy serving.

Win-win.

When we notice what it is that makes us come alive, we're better equipped to embrace our callings. Too often, though, we settle for doing what we've grown to believe that we "should" do, rather than what we're made to do. Serving as a volunteer for the middle school group at church is a fine calling. But if it's not your calling, if you dread every Wednesday night meeting, the kingdom suffers. Starting a business or being an entrepreneur is a genuine calling for many. But if the thought of making a sales call gives you a sinking feeling, it may not be for you. For decades in the church there's been a dangerous myth about calling that says if you get serious about God, God will do something horrible, like call you to be a missionary in Africa. (Cue ominous orchestral music.) But Jesus called fishermen beside Lake Galilee to "fish" for people in the new kingdom he was building. God does not erase who we are when we're called. God honors who we are.

Wild Success Doesn't Mean Fulfillment

Joe was a successful life insurance salesperson.

When I say successful, I mean six-figure successful.

But Joe didn't enjoy his work.

One day Joe and I sat across from each other in rockers on the front porch of my office and discussed the predicament a lot of folks would die for. Despite the good money, Joe wasn't satisfied.

When I asked what he did enjoy, Joe told me it was gardening. During lunch hours he'd escape to Pikes Garden Center to explore various varieties of plants, and in the evenings he'd work in his garden. Joe loved to till the soil, plant seeds, tend the young shoots, fertilize them, watch them grow, and trim them. On the weekends Joe was taking a Master Gardener course. He enjoyed the process of planting and tending and growing a garden. Joe even bartered with me for my coaching services by creating a landscape plan for our home.

Win-win.

As Joe continued to sell insurance, he'd steal away every chance he got to work in his garden. When the passion had grown and was about to burst inside him, Joe resigned his job and began gardening full time. He completed his coursework and became a Master Gardener. Passionate and charismatic, Joe was invited by DIY Network to host a show called *Fresh from the Garden*. Today, as the executive producer and host of the award-winning PBS series *Growing a Greener World*, Joe is one of the country's most recognized and trusted personalities in gardening and sustainability. He's appeared on NBC's *Today*, ABC's *Good Morning America*, The Weather Channel, and more. Joe is doing what he was made to do.

In the course of our conversations and other intentional discernment, Joe had identified three windows through which he came alive: the *what, how,* and *when.*

The *what,* for Joe, was his passion for plants. The *how* was the dirt-under-the-fingernails labor of working with plants. His hands were suited for it. The *when* was not something Joe was always in tune with. He enjoyed the process so much, in fact, that he lost track of all time when he did it. The work seemed to transport him into another time and space.

Sometimes what makes us come alive isn't serving a particular people group. Sometimes we recognize our calling when something that we're doing is what vivifies us—bring us to life. As we give ourselves to an activity or place or people, we discover that we're more alive as we embrace it. That was true for my friend Joe. It's also true for my son, Joshua.

Unquantifiable Vivification

When I watch Joshua skateboard, I'm struck both by the sheer marvel of what he's able to do and also the way it makes him come alive. Joshua can pick up his board with his feet and do a 360-degree turn laterally, while at the same time turning the board 360 degrees vertically. It seems to defy physics.

He lights up when he's outside and comes across a set of stairs. Like a pirate who's unearthed buried treasure, Joshua assesses the stairs by feeling them with his hands, then runs to the crest, where he'll fly over them with his board. Often he falls, but then he tackles it again and again and again until he successfully lands it. For him, learning to fall correctly is more important than landing correctly. If he falls well, he'll eventually land the trick. Joshua applies himself to the challenge at hand with the skill he has developed. Jumping seven stairs or doing a particular trick—one which would be death-dealing for others—enlivens my son.

I also think of my friend Jonathan Merritt, a well-known writer. Jonathan earned a degree in business and after graduation worked as a salesperson for a pool chemical company. Because he wanted to write, he started writing and submitting articles to publishers in his spare time. Noticing the ways in which writing made him come alive, Jonathan kept writing. And writing. And writing. He developed his skill, and after he had submitted one hundred articles, he received his first acceptance letter. If he had not been brought to life by the process of writing, he might have given up. Having a passion for something is what keeps us going, even without the reinforcement we seek from others. Not only did Jonathan's articles begin to get accepted, but he wrote a book. And then another. And then another. Today, he's a popular religion columnist.

As Joshua skates and as Jonathan writes, they are both energized by a *what* that makes them come alive. Unlike Jonathan with his writing, Joshua most likely won't ever earn a living from skating. He's not even sure that he'd want to. What I'm encouraging Joshua to do, though, is to look at the *how* of skating that so ignites him. Sometimes identifying the how—the process by which we find satisfaction—leads us in the direction of our calling.

Notice how you do those things that make you come alive. Some creatives discover that whenever they get their hands on raw materials—a lump of clay, a pencil and music staff, a blank writing page—they are vivified. Others have learned that they are most satisfied as they "order" the world around them. This can include everyone from interior designers to home cleaners to project managers responsible for spreadsheets. Still others are invigorated by physical labor. If you're one of those folks who enjoys calculating your taxes, you may find a ministry serving folks who need what gives you life. As you notice the process, the *how* that makes you come alive, it will offer you clues about the further unfolding of your calling.

I see this in my son. When Joshua skateboards, it's not just that he likes to go fast. There are other components that make it a meaningful experience for him. It's a solitary venture, but others are in the periphery. He applies himself to a singular task and finds opportunities to challenge himself. He competes against himself. Little by little he perfects his craft. He embraces a process that allows him to develop courage. As he and I think about how he approaches his work, we've entertained future possibilities that include engineering, construction, writing, or some other artistic venture.

When the "What" Does Not Inspire

Sometimes the *what* of the job we're doing—as a clerical worker or salesperson, as a custodian or CEO—doesn't fire us up the way we might hope. There will be seasons when our co-workers are insufferable, days when spreadsheets do not inspire, and moments when we just don't like our jobs.

But even when we can't change the *what* of our jobs, if there's a strong enough *why*, our experience of it can be transformed.

Many of us can put up with a lot when there is a meaningful *why*. A clear why can breathe new life into a career or hobby that has grown stale.

What are the causes you believe in? What motivates you? What angers you so much that you slam your fist down on the kitchen table? What breaks your heart to the point of tears? What delights you so much that you jump up and down with joy? These are most likely glimpses into your why.

For years my dad wanted to be a pastor, a social worker, or the owner of a Christian bookstore. Instead, he worked for decades as a pipe fitter. And although he was a great pipe fitter, he wrestled with his vocation over a number of years.

A few years back, several years into retirement, my dad confided in me about this chronic wrestling. He explained that decades earlier, when he'd been on a lunch break at Bethlehem Steel, he gazed out over the lake and reckoned with God, reasoning, "God, if this is where you want me, I will stay."

After that, Dad's attitude at work changed. When he was promoted to shop steward, he became responsible for conducting safety meetings. At the end of each meeting he'd invite anyone who'd like to stay to join him for devotions from the *Our Daily Bread* devotional. Soon he became known as the "chaplain."

If a worker was having trouble with his wife, he'd speak with Dad. If he was locked up in jail for driving under the influence, he'd call Dad. My father wasn't paid to do work that breathed life into him, so he found a way to breathe life into it. He found a *why* that transformed his experience of the *what*. It's not coincidental that he was a skilled pipe fitter and welder. He would not have had the opportunity to infuse his work with the same kind of meaning had he been a slacker. My dad found the work that enlivened him in the context of using his gifts and skills.

Dad's experience also reminds me of my friend Vincente, one of our first employees who immigrated to the US. For seven years Vincente worked faithfully for me on every single project he was given. He learned to roast coffee. He landscaped the land around my office. He painted the interior and exterior of my workspace. Vincente was willing to help in any way he could. He'd even stay at our home and care for our dogs while we were away. And when we'd return, we'd always notice some project he'd completed in our absence, such as organizing my tools, landscaping an overgrown corner of our yard, or lay-ing stones for a pathway along a heavily trafficked patch of dirt.

For Vincente, the *what* wasn't so glamorous. But there were *whys* that moved him. First of all, he was earning money to care for his family. Second, he was saving to build a home. Third, he loved me and worked hard to succeed at whatever was offered to him. If you can identify what is most important in your own experience and can make meaningful connections to the work you do, you will come alive.

Out of Time in the Most Wonderful Way

In English, we have just one word for time. Greek has two words that describe different kinds of time. *Chronos* refers to the time on the clock. Between 1:00 and 3:00, two hours will pass. That's chronos. But there's also *kairos* time. *Kairos* is the Greek word for opportunity. That time that you shared an elevator going up forty-seven flights with the woman or man who'd been your hero since childhood, and you were able to have an intelligible conversation? That's kairos.

In the first century, there was a cult that worshiped the Greek god Kairos. The carved idol of this divine being had a horn on it, like the horn of a bull. And part of the worship ritual around this statue was for the worshiper to reach out and "grab the horn." The modern equivalent might be Nike's inspirational "Just Do It" ad campaign! When you're in kairos time, that prime moment, you seize an opportunity in such a way that you are vivified by it. You come alive. In fact, it can almost feel in that moment as if we've entered into another space and time.

In high school, my buddies and I had been driving around when we stopped for coffee at an old-school diner called "Round-the-Clock." Animated, engaged, and possibly a bit high on caffeine, we got into a mind-bending conversation about the reaches of the galaxies. At some point, remembering I had a curfew, I glanced at my watch and was shocked to discover that three hours had passed! I've known other friends who've had a similar experience while oil painting on canvas or producing music in a sound studio. That's kairos time.

When you get an emergency phone call as you're writing a plotline in the second act of a play, you're thrust back into chronos. When the smoke alarm goes off in the kitchen as you're putting the finishing touches on an exquisite meal, you return to chronos. When you're teaching a classroom full of students and someone's cell phone rings, you're back in chronos. That's when you leave the realm of creating and reenter the drudgery of task management.

This is why God was so insistent about resting on the Sabbath, being undistracted in our worship of him, and embracing rest that ushers us into a time of creation and recreation. Although I don't posit myself as a Sabbath-keeper extraordinaire, I am convinced that embracing Sabbath makes us more fruitful and productive throughout the rest of the week.

When do you find yourself losing track of chronos and entering kairos?

For me, it happens in Rwanda.

My Kairos Place

"Where exactly will you be staying?" my wife asked me as I finished packing my suitcase for my first trip to Rwanda.

"After the first night, I'm not sure," I answered, jamming my running shoes into my bag.

"Who will be picking you up at the airport?" she wondered aloud.

"I don't know," I confessed. My tone also communicated that I didn't need to know.

My answers were less than reassuring.

"Will it be safe?"

"I hope so."

That was true.

Though Land of a Thousand Hills had been in operation for two years, this was my first trip to Rwanda. As I was preparing to leave, my wife and others were concerned about my safety.

Me? Not so much.

The unknowns appealed to me.

Confident the Rwandan adventure would work out, I jetted across the Atlantic for a layover in Amsterdam. While stuck in a hotel overnight, I caught a BBC program on the Holocaust. It detailed the story of children in Michigan, decades later, who'd gotten ahold of one of the boxcars from World War II in which human beings had been captured and transported to Auschwitz to their deaths. These schoolchildren asked people they knew to contribute one paperclip each in order to represent each of the lives that were extinguished.

They received paperclips from teachers and coaches, parents and priests, neighbors and friends. They received paperclips from the Governor of Michigan, the President of the United States, and even the Queen of England. The boxcar filled with millions of paperclips served both as a memorial and also as a tangible reminder of what happened when people who might have acted to protect millions did not.

When the show ended, I still wasn't ready to turn in for the night. Opening up my laptop, I began researching more about the people of Rwanda. That's when I discovered, as I mentioned before, that the Tutsis were once known as the "Tutsi Jews," having brought their Jewish faith with them when they emigrated from Ethiopia hundreds of years earlier. Legend says that the queen of Ethiopia brought the Jewish faith back to her country after one of her visits with King Solomon. In fact, when the Belgian priests and colonists arrived to colonize Rwanda in the 1930s, the royal family of Rwanda still practiced Judaism. Yet the Europeans forced them to convert to Christianity.

These two threads of history—the horror of the Jewish Holocaust and the faith history which would precede Rwandan genocide—remained fresh in my mind as my plane coasted toward the airport in Kigali. Glimpsing the famous lush rolling hills of the country I'd grown to love, I was aware how the experience of the people I was about to meet was so eerily similar to that of people in my own Jewish ancestry.

After the plane coasted to a stop on the tarmac, the ground crew wheeled stairs up to the doorway of the plane. As I stepped across the threshold, a blanket of stars stretched across the heavens, and I smelled the sweet smoke of millions of fires burning light and warmth into the night. Crossing the tarmac, I entered a surprisingly modern building and waited for my luggage to appear on the carousel. When I reached the front of the customs line and was asked the purpose of my visit, I confirmed what I'd penciled onto the government form I'd been handed on the plane: business and ministry.

Officially released into the country, I caught a glimpse of a slight man holding a big sign and beaming with an even bigger smile. The sign read "Bishop Jonathan."

My Brother Saidi

When I approached my eager host, a Rwandan man in his fifties, bald-headed, wiry, and full of life, he announced, "I am Saidi, and Tim Schilling said I am to be your brother for these two weeks."

It was the best airport pickup I've ever had.

We loaded my single suitcase into the SUV and set off through the city. People swarmed the streets, some walking and some running. The contagious energy of seeing others bustle about their work, even at night, made me want to work myself.

As we pushed our way through the melee, Saidi and I became fast friends. I shared with him I was a Christian pastor and he shared that he was a Muslim driver. We both had another profession—coffee! Apart from being a driver, Saidi also tended a few hundred coffee trees.

He explained that during the 1950s, his parents had been exiled from Rwanda during the first genocide. "I grew up in the Congo," he shared, "and when I heard about the war starting in 1994, I decided to come to fight alongside the man who is now president, Paul Kagame."

Their base of operations was in the Virunga Mountains, near the guerrillas. They trained hard and learned how to fight well.

"One day," Saidi continued, "we were pursuing the enemy when I saw a woman lying facedown in the dirt. She'd been hacked by a machete. When I turned her over I found a young baby sheltered in her arms. But the mother was dead."

I felt sick hearing firsthand the kind of story of which I'd been aware but had not personalized. Now it was my brother's story. He picked up the baby, strapped the child to his back, and continued through the village, seeking to end the killing.

Saidi described how he had lost seventy family members during the genocide, but the cruel horror had planted a seed of life. The little orphan he'd carried home on his back became his daughter. He would also come to raise one other boy who'd been orphaned.

During the course of the trip, being with Saidi was one of the best gifts I received. One day, not sure if he had a ready answer locked and loaded, I asked Saidi what his goals were in life. Without hesitating, he declared that he wanted to own one hectare of coffee trees for each of his two adopted orphans.

I was impressed. This would cost him $300 US.

When Saidi returned me to the airport a week later, I reached into my pocket and felt the $300 I'd converted into Rwanda dollars that had been unspent. As I left my brother, I offered it to him, saying, "Saidi, this is for your orphans."

Saidi, who had lost seventy family members in the war, fought alongside the warrior-turned-president, and now drove so skillfully, wept.

Although our friendship and exchange was about much more than me, I noticed that in serving the people of Rwanda, I was coming alive. These were, in so many ways, my people: their history resonated with the history of my ancestors. So many Rwandans, like Saidi, were willing to work hard to reclaim their lives and their country. I'd always championed the underdog, and I resonated with their struggles.

In the middle of our trip, Saidi and I—along with a college intern named Sarah from Boston University—set out toward a town called Bukonya. And although the killing had ended, the brokenness was still palpable: many neighbors in Bukonya hadn't spoken to one another in a dozen years.

As we drove up the treacherous, steep mountain roads and dipped back down into the valleys, I was enthralled by the beauty of these hills. As we crested a final hill and began our descent into the valley of Bukonya, I heard the music before I saw the people.

The sound of drums.

The glorious singing.

The frenzied shouts of joy.

As we approached I saw over five hundred people lined up around the washing station ready to greet us. Many had never seen a white man before. The children flocked to touch my hairy arms. (Rwandan men don't have hair on their arms.)

The adults greeted me with their double-handed handshake, shaking my right hand with theirs and grasping my arm with their left. When I asked what this meant, they said it is a sign of trust, an ancient way to say "with two hands we can."

We shared together in a joyful celebration, exchanging greetings and gifts. It was the day I met the people who would become my people.

Enlivened by My People

Two of the most interesting folks I met were a man named Jean and a woman named Clementine. The three of us sat together on the side of a hill as they shared their story with me. The two had grown up together and been childhood friends. Then, when the war began, Jean left the village to be trained by the death squads known as Interahamwe. When he returned, he slaughtered all of Clementine's family, as well as her livestock. Terrified, she went into hiding and, against the odds, survived.

Jean explained that he'd gone to prison when the war ended. Yet before he'd been arrested, he'd torn up all the coffee trees in the area where he'd lived, just as he'd uprooted the lives of his neighbors.

Jean went on to describe the visit of an Anglican bishop who had come to speak of forgiveness and reconciliation. "He said that God could forgive us in Christ if we would confess our sins and ask." Then, more quietly, he added, "He also said that it might be that our neighbors would forgive us as well."

Clementine chimed in to say that when she was all alone, her pastor began talking to her about forgiveness and let her know that soon Jean might be returning home.

"He did come home," Clementine informed me, "and I avoided him."

Her face became serious as she choked out the rest of her story.

"Every time I saw his face in the village, I felt the pain of my mommy and daddy and brothers and sisters being murdered. The pain of what he tried to do to me. Yet I knew I had to let it go to forgive."

The church instructed Clementine about how to be reconciled to this man. Even the government told her she should be reconciled to him.

Clementine explained, "It is only now as we sit together with you over coffee that I am being reconciled."

The government had given both Clementine and Jean a piece of land on which to grow coffee, and they chose to join their parcels together to cultivate the soils, plant seedlings, and harvest the fruit.

As I struggled to process the situation she was describing, Clementine affirmed, "It is better together. If one of us needs to be in the field, the other can watch the children. We work together for coffee, and we work on the problems we have. We talk it out as we work together."

I'd never witnessed any reconciliation so powerful.

As I listened to their stories and got to know not just Jean and Clementine but others as well, I came alive. These people came to be my people. In Rwanda I learned that I could be who I was, use what I had, and get what I could to help a people who I liked.

I was engaged by the deep longing of a people that touched something deep inside my own soul. Perhaps that will be your experience too, but it doesn't have to be. Begin discerning the actions, places, and people that ignite your unique passions. Whether it is a tender place in your soul that weeps with those who weep or a joyful explosion when you rejoice with those who rejoice, that which vivifies you points toward your calling.

1. In the last six to twelve months, what have you done at work, at church, or at play that has made you come alive?

2. Can you remember an experience further back in your past—coursework, a hobby, a service project, something else—in which you felt fully alive?

3. Right now, what is one "next step" you could take toward pursuing that calling in which you feel fully alive?

– 7 –

Bringing Hitchhikers Home for Dinner

Find a People to Serve

"Don't drink, don't smoke, what do you do?" Adam Ant's 1982 lyrics from the song "Goody Two Shoes" were a fitting mantra for the home and church in which I was raised as a fundamentalist Baptist.

In our church, not only were we not supposed to be listening to Adam Ant, the front page of our hymnal also announced that we abstained from the purchase and use of intoxicating drink and tobacco and also a myriad of other "sinful" pastimes.

That my family attended a church that was "hard-core" Christian was no accident. Though my dad had been raised without regular worship experience, his father had held on to many of the legalistic aspects of Orthodox Judaism. When my dad became a Christian, he chose an ilk that had plenty of rules as well. My dad was all in. When he set his mind to something, he was going to do it better than anyone else. The same reservoir of pride and excellence that fueled his work as a pipe fitter drove his faith.

But if Dad's adherence to the rules was tight, his love for people was generous and free. He joined the other Baptist men who visited the local prison to conduct Bible studies and worship services. Each Sunday morning he'd drive the church bus to pick up kids from the inner city and bring them to church. When the Indiana snow piled high, he'd always make sure that Mrs. Lewis, the widow five doors down, was safe and cared for. My dad loved people well.

That Time My Dad Was *Not* Being Held Hostage

When I was nine years old, I was putting the finishing touches on a custom-built Lego truck, right before dinner, when Dad walked through the back door with a man I'd never seen before. He carried a big backpack with a sleeping bag roll strapped to the bottom, which I thought was pretty cool. He had a scruffy, light brown beard, and his hair was longer than anyone I'd ever seen in the pews at church. While I was waiting to hear whether my dad was being held hostage or if this guy had just been released from prison, Dad simply showed the stranger where he could drop his backpack and wash up, and announced, "Marian, we have company." Over dinner I learned that when Dad had pulled over to offer a lift to this hitchhiker, he'd discovered that the man was hungry. So we gained a guest.

As we pursue our callings, many of us will discover that we've been called to serve a particular people. Sometimes the people we're called to serve are those whose lives look a lot like our own. If you grew up in an urban neighborhood, or worked on a farm, or conquered addiction, you might be called to people whose stories resonate with your own. But we're often called to those whose lives look different.

One couple I know, who'd both grown up in solid, stable homes, were clear that they were called to open their home to children in the foster care system. My dad was called to folks who were down on their luck. One nurse I know has poured her life into children infected with HIV/AIDS. A group of men near Washington, DC, have all invested in the nation's senators and representatives for decades. Another friend has been called to befriend and serve people with disabilities. I even know of a guy whose calling involves ministering to race car drivers! As you survey your past, who were those folks that you enjoyed serving? Were they in a hospice or a hospital? Were they working in cubicles or driving pickup trucks? Were they wearing cleats or carrying textbooks? Begin to notice the kinds of people you've already served.

Finding My People

After high school I attended Cedarville University. While there, I found myself rebelling against the legalistic theology I had been raised with. I often drank beer, smoked pot with buddies, and visited with the townies. Though I wasn't walking the narrow path, I still took delight in helping others. I shared the gospel with friends, visited the nursing home, and became a "big brother" to a young family without a father. My calling found a way of breaking through even in the midst of my doing some pretty sinful stuff. But Cedarville was not some Big Ten party school. In fact, during the second semester of my sophomore year, I was about to be kicked out of school when I was drawn back from the edge. Against all odds, Pat Bates, Cedarville's dean of women, recognized something in me that was worth redeeming. She stood in the gap for me and convinced other administrators to allow me to stay at Cedarville.

Slowly, God began to mature me.

During my first year at Richmont Graduate University studying for a master's in counseling, I was selected to be the class chaplain. Five years after I graduated, I'd discover that the kinds of beliefs and behaviors that make people effective or ineffective in their interpersonal relationships have the same effect professionally. That's when I moved into doing more professional consulting work. This was the season when I was able to help a lot of people—through individual Lifeswork coaching and also corporate contracts—discover the kind of work for which they were made.

And in that season of rumination and reevaluation when the insurance company canceled my contract, I noticed that I was being called not necessarily to a "thing"—a new business or position—but that I was being called to serve a particular community of people. For me, that was a local church congregation.

Serving the Theologically Interested

I had a coaching client once who'd been working full time for Ravi Zacharias, an author, speaker, and Christian apologist. Bill enjoyed his work with Ravi Zacharias Ministries but had an inkling that he was being called to something else. As we spent time together in conversation, Bill's passion for the writings of C. S. Lewis came tumbling out.

Specifically, he derived endless fulfillment when he had the opportunity to serve people who were interested in the life and work of C. S. Lewis. I watched him come to life when given the opportunity to answer questions about Lewis or suggest books whose substance might help others facing challenges in their lives. I saw Bill courageously make room in his life for this deep passion to breathe and grow.

A few years ago, I received this letter from Bill:

Jonathan, don't know if you remember me, but I met with you about five years ago. During our conversation you suggested that my passion seemed to be connected with my interest in C. S. Lewis, so perhaps I should consider further developing some of the presentations that I had put together related to his life and writings.

I wanted to let you know that I followed through with your suggestions and since that time have formed a partnership with The C. S. Lewis Institute (www.cslewisinstitute.org) to form The C. S. Lewis Institute Atlanta. In the last four years we have conducted ten conferences in partnership with churches and various organizations. We have also had about forty people complete The Fellow Program, our one-year intensive discipleship initiative. On top of this I regularly have opportunities to speak on subjects related to C. S. Lewis.

I am informing you of all these details to say thanks for your wise input about moving in this direction. I believe the Lord used our conversations in my life.

By the way, about two weeks ago I met with some young church planters in the Vinings area who told me about your coffee shop on the river. I have had a couple of relaxing visits already. Love to get together sometime soon and hear about how you are doing.

Blessings,
Bill Smith

I can't describe what a gift it was to be allowed that peek into what had transpired when Bill pursued his calling.

Not a Wild Goose Chase

Remember Cassidy, a woman in my congregation who'd admitted that she really didn't enjoy the women she was serving? That was an opportune moment for her to recognize that although she was doing "good work," she hadn't yet landed on her own true calling. These weren't her people to serve.

Even as I say that Cassidy had not yet discovered her true calling, I want to extend one caution. I've known people who've approached this business of identifying their calling, or pursuing their life's work, as a guessing game akin to the Parker Brothers board game Clue. These earnest seekers move through life as if God has hidden their true calling on cards in a small envelope that they must discern through random guessing until they at last ascertain what was hidden. Instead of discovering it was "Miss Scarlet, with the candlestick, in the library," they're hoping God will deliver carefully engraved tablets just as revelatory: "needy children, with heavy equipment to dig wells, in Africa." (It would be awesome if it was that easy, right?)

I want to suggest that God is much more gracious than that. God is not interested in hiding anything from you. Rather, as you pay attention to the kinds of people and work and places that do vitalize you, you can recognize and claim those as being gifts of God.

Giving and Receiving

As you do discover the folks you've been called to serve—not grudgingly but joyfully—I suspect you'll also discover that God's pleasure in connecting you was never meant to be unilateral. Rather, I expect you'll find that you are mutually served and blessed. For while there's an individualistic element to this business of embracing your calling, God's grand design is so much more expansive and purposeful than helping you to "find your thing." It's not all about you. (Hopefully, this isn't coming as a surprise.) There is an interconnectedness to a wide variety of callings and how we serve people from our heart. As we serve with passion we build community.

When I first met my friend Paul, I was walking my dog through his neighborhood and he was sitting on the porch of his motor home. We struck up a conversation, and Paul ended up being one of my coaching clients! At the time, Paul was working with Cornerstone Support, developing software for collection agencies. While for many people this sounds like the least sexy of all callings, it's perfect for Paul. He loves to design, create, and find fresh solutions. But there was even more for Paul. He set a goal to travel the nation with his family in their motor home. He began to write a screenplay. He also continues his work with Cornerstone Support. And while I'd imagined that developing software was a solitary calling, I discovered that Paul really enjoys the team with whom he works. His company offers one of the best employee benefit programs I know of, treating its workers with respect. In turn, they treat their employer with respect and enjoy serving him. They have developed a strong, healthy community. These are Paul's people—not just because he "serves" them but because the relationships are ones that are mutual.

Who are the ones who you have blessed and who have blessed you in return?

On Not Being a Rich White Guy

Before I first went to Rwanda, my friend Bob, another social entrepreneur, met me for coffee to catch up and give me some pointers. Specifically, he encouraged me to go with open heart and hands, ready to receive from the people of Rwanda.

When he began, "Don't be the rich white guy," I'll admit that I couldn't really see a way around that one.

But he continued: "Don't be the rich white guy who's going to go in to fix things. Go with the mindset of creating community."

Though I knew he was right, in that moment as I was sitting in the coffee shop sipping a tall soy latte, I couldn't know how Bob's wisdom would unfold.

And although I wish I'd not had to learn under such dire circumstances, a few years later the comical Warner Brothers cartoon lightbulb flashed on over my head while standing in a circle of twelve farmers from Mbilima.

I was traveling with my trusted associate Manny Gatare, one of the amazing people who makes Land of a Thousand Hills work in Rwanda, for Rwandans. He was the one who had relationships with the farmers who work with us. And during this visit, these farmers were up in arms because of a slow harvest season. They weren't able to produce the quantity and quality of coffee they usually grew.

Although I'd not planned on sharing our business woes, I heard myself explaining to these hardworking farmers the troubles I'd been facing. We'd had a container of coffee, worth $150,000, stolen during shipment. And we had another container we'd expected to be buying sold out from under us. As they listened to what the company had been facing, their faces softened.

One of the leaders of the group expressed their genuine sorrow and asked if they could pray for us. Then a dozen Rwandan men circled up, joined hands, and prayed for me, for Manny, and for our company. After praying, they patted me on the back and wished me well. And while I'd received other support from friends back home during that most trying moment of my professional career, there was something about other "coffee guys" supporting me that gave me courage to continue to fight for the business and for them.

I knew that many folks back home saw me as the person who was serving them. But the understanding, support, and encouragement I received from these brothers convinced me otherwise. These were my people, and our commitment to one another was mutual.

Believe me, the power dynamics between the "rich white guy" and a handful of farmers eking out a living in a country so recently devastated by war were not lost on me. But I also understand the necessity of mutuality. If the people among whom you've been called to serve are never given the opportunity to serve you, you will rob them of their dignity. God never intended for relationships to be unilateral. If you're not convinced, notice the consistent witness of Jesus among a variety of people and groups. Mary washed his feet. The disciples protected him by shuttling him away from the cloying crowds. Embracing the value of mutuality, Jesus received the hospitality of his friends.

When you find your people to serve, you can expect to experience mutual care for one another.

Hoop Group Love

One of my wife's closest friends is a woman I'll call Jill. For months, the two of them gathered with one other friend, Sandy, on Monday nights. One night when these friends were discussing the need for hope, Jill accidentally said "hoop," so their group became known as the "Hoop Group"!

A few weeks back Jill was facing some seismic challenges in her life. Some of the Christian promises she'd believed in hadn't yet been realized the way she'd hoped and expected them to be. She was depressed and despondent. Jill had texted my wife, Brenda, earlier in the day to let her know that she was done with God for a while. And though the other two went ahead and met, they felt a deep uneasiness for their friend.

So even though it was already 11:00 at night, they hopped into Sandy's yellow VW Bug and drove the fifteen miles to Jill's home. Pounding on her door, they waited for an answer. When Jill's husband cracked the door open, Sandy announced, "We're here to see Jill and we aren't taking no for an answer!" By this time it was after midnight. Left with no other choice, he opened the door and let them in.

The three women gathered on the couch together under blankets, cracked open a bottle of wine, shared their hearts, laughed, cried, and prayed together. (A typical night for the hoopsters.)

The next Sunday at church, Jill's husband Joe stood up during the prayers of the people and offered discretely, "This week Jesus showed up at our house."

You can bet that when my wife Brenda faces a challenge, Jill and Sandy will be there with a bottle of wine. (And I'll let them in at midnight.)

The Naval Commander's People
Aren't Who You Think

On September 10, 1928, Jean Vanier was born in Paris to a highly decorated World War I Major-General veteran who was serving as a Canadian ambassador in Paris. Much of Vanier's childhood was spent traveling the world with his parents until World War II erupted. Living in Paris at the time, he and his mother would assist concentration camp survivors. Later they were forced to flee as the Nazi regime invaded. Assisting his mother bred in Jean Vanier a deep love and passion for those in need.

Vanier spent the remainder of the war studying at an English naval academy, training for a future in the Royal Navy. He rose through the ranks to become a well-decorated Navy Commander.

When he returned to Paris in 1964, Vanier visited his priest and friend, Father Thomas Phillippe. During that visit, Vanier was horrified by the conditions of the mental health asylum they'd visited just south of the city. Vanier witnessed the residents of the asylum wandering in meaningless circles for hours on end, without proper care, love, or stimulation.

Moved to action, Vanier purchased a small house in Trosly-Breuil and continued to think about what he'd seen. These weren't men with any sort of psychosis that made them a danger to society, as the word *asylum* might imply. They were men who'd been born with developmental disabilities. Recognizing their undeniable humanity and inherent dignity, Vanier took a chance and invited two of them to live with him.

This small community of friends would grow and later be-come known as L'Arche, French for "the ark," like Noah's float-ing house of rescue and safety. L'Arche now has 147 homes in thirty-five countries around the globe. Today an international advocate for those with intellectual disabilities, Vanier tells countless stories of the people who enter these communities—as resident or as helper—to discover love and healing. He also describes the delight he experiences receiving food and drink and communion from these brothers and sisters with whom he shares a mutual love.

In *Becoming Human*, Vanier writes, "Communion is mu-tual trust, mutual belonging; it is the to-and-fro movement of love between two people where each one gives and each one receives. Communion is not a fixed state, it is an ever-growing and deepening reality."[6]

As you flesh out your calling, your gifts and resources meet the needs of others, and their gifts and resources meet yours. When this ceases to be the case, relationships become transactions. Not only does work become a commodity, but people do as well. Rather than enjoying a community, you create an "exchange."

Are there relationships in your life right now where you're enjoying a rich sense of community and belonging? These may be meaningful markers pointing toward the ones to whom you have been called.

Holy Mutuality

Rowan Williams is the former Archbishop of Canterbury. He has shared that before he goes to visit someone, whether that be in an English village or in the heart of the Congo, he asks God, "What needs do you want to meet through me for them and through them for me?" Similarly, Walter Brueggeman and Peter Block discuss the dynamic of community in which a mutual giving and receiving of gifts reinforces our sense of citizenship rather than consumerism. As citizens, we each take responsibility for our community. As consumers, we do not. Communities seek to solve their own problems rather than outsourcing them. They police themselves; they heal themselves. For example, an adolescent facing crisis isn't just outsourced to a counselor, but rather the community helps and supports the entire family. In a community, you don't wait for the government to fix the roads; you fix them yourselves. I found this to be true in Rwanda, where once a month everyone works to better the local community. The roads are literally fixed by the village members. Communities value the contributions of everyone.

The way in which you embrace a people through your calling will lead to either citizenship or consumerism. Consumers expect to receive from a giver. The receiver then becomes no more than a client, customer, or even worse, target audience. In fact, some churches even commission a "first impressions" team whose job is to ensure an optimal "customer experience" for visitors. Yet how much richer and more humanizing would it be to send out people with the gift of hospitality to welcome and build relationships with newcomers, acknowledging that each newcomer has something to offer to the community.

I confess that I've made mistakes in this area. I mentioned earlier that a few years ago I became aware that while I'd mastered the "entrepreneur" half of "social entrepreneur," I'd let "social" lag behind. I fell into the trap of behaving as savior to the community, rather than as a member of it. Yet my conviction about building community with the people I was called to serve—if they were indeed integral to my calling—is what moved me to action, to rebuild relationships.

As I became aware, I began to notice the strength of relational investment among others in our organization as well. For three years we tried to establish a coffee presence in Haiti. The agronomist and collaborative trade director we'd hired there, who'd grown up in the same village as some of our farmers, would strut around in a business suit and dress shoes. Time and time again he'd fail to plant the seedlings we asked him to plant. Money followed after money, $60,000 over two years, without any investment on the part of the people he managed. It wasn't just this fellow. Another in-country partner, a nonprofit from the United States, had been tasked to provide leadership. Not only did they fail to do this, but they also failed to bring coffee-buying partners to the table, as agreed. As I realized that our relationships with both those in the village and also the NGO were one-sided, it became clear that we weren't co-laboring. It soon became clear to me that our work there had come to an end.

From the moment Land of a Thousand Hills was conceived, we've been about two things: making good coffee and doing good. All our efforts have been poured into working and helping others. We've built a school for five hundred children. We've constructed an orphanage. We've gathered up three children and taken them under our wings by providing housing, food, and education. Though they still live in Rwanda, Brenda and I are their parents. We've bought and distributed nearly one thousand coffee bicycles and over five hundred goats. But all this work through our nonprofit, called the Do Good Initiative, has not achieved the kind of traction we've seen with the coffee business itself. I know that the charitable things we have done through the Do Good Initiative have been needed. But although we've helped widows, orphans, and strangers in our midst, this sector of our work has not resonated with me the way the business has.

The business, however, has been where I've found a place to serve and be served. When our collaborative trade director, Manny Gatare, and I get together, we are dangerous! (Dangerously good.) When I gather with our team at Ruli—Aimee, Geraldine, Alex, and Gloriose—I come alive.

And since I believe I mentioned that it's not all about me, I recognize that a vibrant kind of collaborative has formed among that same group. These friends who were once four single adults, disenfranchised children of the genocide, have become a team in both business and living. All four have married and have children. They care for each other, and they also care for me as I care for them. They remind me again and again that my people to serve are workers and craftsmen.

Among workers, I want to be working with those who are driven to cover the same ground I do. When friends want to run with me—literally tie on some running shoes and hit the pavement—I warn them that they need to keep pace with me. I'm not apt to slow down to drag someone along, but I'll look to the left and to the right and chat with those at my side as we run and work together. Intrinsic to who I am is a drive to see progress. I want to see people thrive and grow and move. Within my sphere of work with Land of a Thousand Hills, where I have the opportunity to dabble in lots of areas, I take special delight in creative visioning, so that we can serve the world together.

I delight in serving those who are my people.

As you pursue your calling, identify the people whom you are *delighted* to serve. Consider your history and notice any patterns that emerge. Return to those moments when you were most fully alive and—as if in a frozen frame of a film—look around you at the other faces in the room, on the bus, in the field, or in the classroom.

You will delight in serving those who are your people.

1. Over the years, who are the folks you've enjoyed serving? Were they folks who lived on the world's margins? Were they wearing business suits? Were they speaking English? Were they physically healthy? Notice who you've enjoyed serving.

2. What are the relationships in your life in which you're experiencing the blessedness of community and mutuality?

3. Right now, what is one "next step" you could take?

– 8 –

The Man Who Murdered
Your Family

Growing Little by Little

I fixed my gaze on my father's rugged hand caressing my mother's smooth, weathered one. She'd been in ICU for two weeks, suffering from pneumonia, influenza, and a ruptured intestine. As all five of us grown children were crammed into her hospital room, I thought about all that had been exchanged between those two hands. Every day of their sixty-five-year marriage, Dad had brewed Mom a cup of tea and taken it to her in bed. That daily little deposit of faithfulness is one of many between them that accrued into what has become a solid marriage together. It is a relationship that has been built day in and day out over the decades. And I've been an eyewitness who will vouch that it hasn't always been easy! (Golden men can be, shall we say, strong-willed.) And yet little by little, tea cup by tea cup, they built what has become a marriage I admire and strive, in many ways, to emulate.

This systematic "little by little" approach is what my Rwandan friends call *bahora bahora*. Little by little. *Bahora bahora*, you grow coffee. *Bahora bahora*, you raise your children. *Bahora bahora*, you transform a community through coffee. This gradual rhythm of building over time is a stark contrast to *vooba vooba*. *Vooba* means "quickly." When evil is recognized to be present, it ought to be uprooted *vooba vooba*. When one asks forgiveness for committing a wrong against another, he asks *vooba vooba*. When a hungry child needs to be fed, she's cared for *vooba vooba*. But creating a marriage that stretches across decades, or establishing a reconciled community where there was once deep brokenness, requires a steadfast *bahora bahora* commitment to fidelity in relationship.

Learning from Seraphine and Onesphore

Two months ago, in the parish church of Kiryamo, a large brick building situated adjacent to the Forgiveness School we'd built for local children, I sat down with Seraphine and Onesphore. Onesphore was a somber man with a strong, muscular frame. The expression on his face reminded me of that moment of early dusk or dawn when a grayness in the atmosphere blurs the line between night and day. Seraphine, a beautiful woman with radiant, smooth chocolate skin, broad features, and a contagious smile, appeared at once weathered by the world's storms and strong enough to endure them. Life seemed to be bursting forth from Seraphine.

As we settled in to sit in a small circle, I asked if I could pray. Both agreed, and I offered, "Jesus, the great Reconciler, please be with us. Let me learn from these two friends and continue to bring healing between them and in this community."

Gently, Seraphine began, "We grew up in the same village, and for a time, we all were one. We worked together in the village, growing our food, tending our coffee trees, raising our children, and going to church together." Her face falling, she added, "Then the change happened."

Seraphine began to describe the ugly chaos which had unfolded in her country. "The vicious talks, the radio programs, even some of the preaching in church was tearing down the Tutsi people. Yet so many of us were of both Tutsi and Hutu origin that I didn't think it would affect us."

"Then the men," she continued, "including Onesphore, left for training. When they came back they were changed. There was a vengeance in them. They started killing first on the outskirts of the village, then in the village itself. They killed my father and my husband—one day they left for work and they did not return."

Onesphore, wearing rubber flip-flop sandals, looked down at his dusty feet as Seraphine spoke.

She explained her own survival. "I hid in the back stable where we kept our cows. Day after day I hid and ate the grass that was nearby, and eventually it ended. But my grief had just started. I had no man in my life; no one to love and be loved by. My father was gone, my husband was gone, and all the work on the farm was left to me."

When the violence ended, perpetrators were imprisoned for a period. But then the government suggested that the murderers be released to return to their villages to help care for the women who remained. A representative from the government stood at Seraphine's doorstep and asked her, "Could you begin to forgive?"

Onesphore lifted his eyes. As I wondered what it must feel like to bear such a weight of shame, he interjected as if reading my mind.

"Am I ashamed to share with you now? No, the time for shame would have been when I was doing the killing. Have I asked her to forgive me? Yes, and I ask her every day. My dying words on my mouth will be, 'Will you forgive me?'"

Onesphore continued to describe his crimes. "Yes, I killed; I took the machete with the other men and I killed her husband. I hacked him blow by blow, and then went on to the next. I knew it was wrong, but something came over me."

I felt sick, imagining what it would be like to hear the slaying of my spouse recounted in my presence.

"When we knew the war would be ending, and that we were losing," Onesphore explained, "we then started tearing up the crops and the coffee trees because we didn't want Kagame and the RPF to have them."

He then described discovering forgiveness through Jesus Christ while he was in prison, explaining that although he knew he'd been forgiven by Jesus, he didn't expect Seraphine to forgive him.

When Onesphore was released, he began the long walk home wondering if he'd be beaten and killed by villagers, as he felt he deserved. Head hung low as he approached the village, he heard what sounded like singing. Perhaps, he thought, it was shouts of revenge from those about to kill him.

But the singing and shouting were not about revenge.

"The closer I got," Onesphore told me, "the louder the sound became. Then I heard that it wasn't the frenzied shouts that we made in our killing, but rather I was hearing songs to a God that sustains and heals and forgives."

Sitting in a circle among the other villagers, Onesphore confessed to murdering several people who'd been known and loved in the village, even detailing how he'd done it: surrounding Seraphine's husband, knocking him down, and doing what he could never forgive himself for.

Of Seraphine, he confessed, "I could barely look at her eyes." But when he did, he did not see hatred.

"When I looked in her eyes," Onesphore explained, "I saw light. I saw that she was able to forgive."

I breathed in the sacredness of the moment. After we were all silent for several minutes, I spoke.

Recognizing the horrendous burden my friend would be carrying throughout his days, I asked, "What brings you relief?"

Onesphore didn't hesitate. "Helping her in any way I can. If she needs her crops harvested or a hole in her roof fixed, I like to help. I do for her what her husband and father would have done."

What Seraphine said next sunk into my deep places: "It is still hard, but we work it out little by little in the garden as we work together."

Little by little.

The way forgiveness works is *bahora bahora*.

Finding Your Calling *Bahora Bahora*

Little by little is also the way your calling unfolds. Though sometimes you'll be lit up with passion and emotion, more often you'll be plodding *bahora bahora*, lurching in the right direction. Friedrich Nietzsche wrote, "The essential thing 'in heaven and in earth' is, apparently . . . that there should be long obedience in the same direction, there thereby results, and has always resulted in the long run, something which has made life worth living."[7] This faithful long obedience is too often a lost art in a society in which we have starter homes and starter spouses, where we change churches as if we're choosing between movie theaters on Friday nights.

I recently saw a book called *Three Minutes to a Better Marriage*. Convinced, by Nietzsche and others, that what makes life worth living is hammered out—God willing—over six and seven decades, I wasn't tempted to buy it! Many of us have been conditioned to reduce emotional maturity to seven simple steps or to see mentoring as a transaction that can be completed over the span of a twelve-month course.

Convinced that *bahora bahora* is what builds that which lasts, I've seen real transformation happen among a group of men who met one evening per month for years, pouring themselves into one another's lives and even caring for each other's kids. *Bahora bahora* is the songwriter who commits to pen one fresh lyric every single day. It also reminds me of author Lauren Winner. In her book *Girl Meets God*, Winner describes confessing to her Anglican priest that she slept with her boyfriend . . . again. The priest reminded her that although she was now lamenting having slept with him just once, when she first had come to confess she'd been sleeping with him quite often. This pastor helped her to realize she was getting better bit by bit.[8]

Little by little we become more holy.

Little by little we craft lyrics to entire songs.

Little by little we become proficient at our callings.

As you pursue your calling there will come a day, a moment, when you have to make a decision. Not just any decision but a commitment decision. A commitment decision is a decision to pursue your calling that can't be easily revoked. It is what some call "pulling a Cortés."

No Turning Back

In 1519, Captain Hernán Cortés, a Spanish conquistador, landed in Veracruz to begin his great conquest of the land that is now Mexico. Upon arriving, he issued to his men this absurd and inconceivable order: burn the ships. With it, Cortés removed any possibility of retreat or withdrawal.

Retreat is easy when you have the option.

In the areas of our lives that are the most difficult, many of us harbor in our minds some sort of exit strategy that brings us comfort. It's our "just in case" safety net. In our difficult marriages, our conflicted churches, or our burdensome jobs, we leave some wiggle room that will release us from our obligations if things get too hard.

But Cortés was on a mission. And he knew that the only way to keep his men—and possibly himself!—from quitting was to remove that option from the table. Retreat was not an option. He forced himself and his men into a position where they would either succeed or die.

To achieve the level of success we each desire, there are times when each of us needs to burn the ships.

What are your ships? What are you hanging on to so that you have an easy exit if you need one? Is it your bank account? Your part-time job? The life-depleting career with the fat paycheck? Your singleness when you recognize the call to marry? Or your harmful marriage when you know it should end? And once you identify that thing, what makes it so hard to burn? Fear of the unknown? Fear of hard work? Fear of being perceived as a failure?

I think of Seraphine and Onesphore. If either one of them had the financial or relational resources to start afresh anyplace else, I have to imagine that both would consider it. But for better or for worse, by circumstance more than by choice, neither one had an exit strategy.

As you pursue your calling, pull a Cortés. Burn the ships. Make the commitment decision.

That may mean quitting your day job. (For some, it may not!)

It may mean making a financial investment in your calling that stretches you beyond your comfort level.

Perhaps it means investing in the kind of education or training that will allow you to pursue your calling.

It may mean making a geographic move.

As you decide to be serious about your calling, you will continue to go after it *bahora bahora*.

The Way Goals Are Reached

When Brenda and I signed the contract on our home in 1992, I didn't expect that it would ever be paid off. The distant date recorded on our twenty-year mortgage made us feel like we wouldn't own it outright until the next millennium. (Oh, wait . . .) This is why it amazes me that today, our home is paid off. And we did it *bahora bahora*.

That there was a structure in place—a monthly coupon book reminding us to pay the mortgage—made it possible. If it had been up to me to make those payments when I felt like it, or as I remembered, or when I had some extra money in my pocket, we'd be living in a refrigerator box today. The negligible amount of principal that we chipped away at each month hardly seemed worth the effort. But because there was a structure in place, we paid it off. Little by little.

When plodding behind the lawn mower, cutting the grass, seems entirely meaningless, you can notice what you've accomplished as you push it next to the previous row that's been cut. Or if you're a weightlifter who adds just one extra pound every week, by the end of a year you'll be sliding fifty extra pounds onto the bar. Though we don't recognize the change in every moment, it's nonetheless happening bit by bit.

My own routine at the gym, though sometimes intermittent, is one to which I always seem to return. Each time it's as if my body recalls the distant memory of the process. I shove what I need into my bag without even thinking: workout clothes, iPod, work clothes. I no longer have to think about it. Stepping onto the floor of the weight room, my body begins the same workout I've done since I was sixteen: three sets of bench presses, three sets of incline, three sets of decline, and three sets of triceps. The fact that after more than three decades, my body instinctively returns to this known routine eliminates even my most creative excuses when I don't feel like doing what I know my body needs to do.

My friends in Rwanda live with this determination.

When many chose to tear down banana trees in order to plant coffee trees, they'd made a commitment decision. They'd burned the boats. When those trees grow during pre-harvest season, these farmers must tend to them. When the time is right, they must prune them and pick the cherries. The annual structure has been imposed, and they must live by it. If a Rwandan farmer wakes up in the morning and doesn't feel like working, or is in want of encouragement, or questions his choice to become a coffee farmer, or wonders whether the reward for his work will come forth at the end of the season, the work still needs to be done.

Bahora bahora it is.

As a child you may have noticed a person you hoped to emulate. You may have dreamed of being a world-renowned ballerina, a brave firefighter, or the president of the United States. And from the perspective of a child, those glamorous "callings" seemed almost magical. What you didn't see, as a child, were all the baby steps that led to the feature on the cover of *Sports Illustrated* or a photo in the local paper or an oath sworn on inauguration day. You didn't see the hours of stretching and training in the dance studio. You didn't know about the torn ligaments and muscles. You weren't aware that the firefighter in the paper lost one of his buddies in the fire he survived. You didn't see the president pulling all-nighters at campaign headquarters.

Whatever your calling, you begin by taking the first small step.

Then another.

And then another.

Baby Steps in the Dark

Sometimes your feet will fall on well-lit paths. Other times, you'll be walking in the dark. A well-known editor friend of mine, Victor Oliver, once shared with me this Danish proverb: "A friend is someone that sings the song of your heart when you have forgotten the words."

As you live your calling, there will come a time when despite your commitment decision and despite the structure you've put in place, you feel like quitting. Giving up. Going away. These are the moments when our friends, our co-laborers, must step in and sing what our silent voices have forgotten.

If you are a Rwandan farmer and you aren't tending your trees, a neighbor will eventually come to see if you are all right. She'll investigate to find out whether you need help from a doctor or whether you just need a kick in the pants to get out of bed.

Each of us needs the same.

When I first started my coaching and consulting business, I'd chat each morning with my friend (and CPA) Bob Gard.

"Bob, how's it going?"

"What is your biggest challenge today?"

"How can I help?"

"How can I pray for you?"

Though we both worked something like soloists, we recognized the importance of collaboration.

There was also a season when I questioned the "success" of our little church, St. Peter's Place. When my friend David and I were sharing a beer one evening, he asked, "What if the sole purpose of the church was for you to meet your son and adopt him?" David's wondering did resonate in my own heart.

I also recall sharing a relational difficulty with my friend Eric, a deacon postulant in the church. As we each held a warm cup of coffee in our hands, Eric would listen and answer, "Well, like you told me," and proceed to parrot back the exact words I'd shared with him when he'd been facing a challenge. I needed Eric to remind me of the song of my heart.

If you wait to seek out these friends when you need them, it will be too late. You have to dig your wells before you are thirsty. So who are your traveling companions? Who do you want to grow old with? Who do you want to carry your coffin? You cannot pursue your calling alone.

The apostle Paul wrote to the church in Corinth and reminded them that "we are labourers together with God" (1 Cor. 3:9 KJV). We are co-laborers beside Christ, with God. The word *co-laborers* is the Greek word for synergy. And though the word is thrown about a lot today, many of us still aren't sure what it means! The German psychotherapist Fritz Perls wrote about synergy and holism. Holism is the psychological and spiritual premise that the whole is greater than the sum of the parts. A holist believes that together we are quantifiably more than we'd be if we added all our separate work together. A reductionist, however, sees each individual as an island without need of others; our work together is no more than the work we'd accomplish alone.

And yet as members of one body, as co-laborers, our work requires others. In the late 1800s, the medical doctor and psychotherapist Alfred Adler identified three tasks to life: eking out our existence on this earth, laboring with others to build community, and establishing monogamous relationships. We weren't built to function alone, and as we pursue our callings, as we work toward them little by little, we do it within the context of community.

The author of Hebrews wrote that the One who endured the cross—the most courageous of callings!—did so "for the joy set before him" (Heb. 12:2 NIV). Jesus Christ kept his eyes on the prize in the most difficult of circumstances.

When you're living into your calling little by little, stay focused on the vision of what you're called to. Keep the main thing the main thing.

Looking toward the Future

As you purpose to take small steps toward the calling that has your name on it, you might create a vision board. You might tear out the pages of *National Geographic* or *Scientific American* magazines and pin those to a bulletin board you can see every day. Or you might have two friends that you meet with every year and talk to on the phone every month. Those friends might ask you at the beginning of every phone call, "What baby step did you take this month to pursue your calling?" Perhaps you'll commit to submitting one piece of work—a film script, a poem, a song, a sculpture—into a contest two times every year. Whatever your calling, embrace tangible practices which become the small steps that propel you forward.

At the beginning of this past year I sat down with my Evernote app and created a vision board. I pasted images of what and who I was aspiring to be and accomplish. Among other things, it included images of a healthy man, a family adventure, and . . . sheep. There's a story behind the sheep, but I did know that if I was ever going to reach the goal I have of raising sheep, I'd need to keep my eyes on what I hoped to accomplish. And although I didn't review the vision board every day, throughout the year I'd look at it, remember my intentions for the year, and then live my life accordingly.

Sustaining Our True Callings

In my work as a social entrepreneur, I get really fired up about business. And although Land of a Thousand Hills was benefiting Rwandan farmers, about a year ago I realized that I hadn't invested deeply enough in getting to know our friends in Rwanda. During my most recent visit, I purposed to spend as much time on relationships, building friendships with our farmers, as I did on the requisite *vooba vooba*. As I sat and talked and listened to Rwandan friends, I was revitalized.

I confess that there have been weeks and months when I was so caught up in the daily grind—pun intended—of Land of a Thousand Hills coffee company that I lost track of the future we'd set out to achieve. In fact, before the trip to Rwanda when I was able to connect with women and men there, I'd felt like giving up.

When I'd arrived, I'd given up hope in the business and even given up on God. Yet as I was traveling on the road from Bukonya, drinking in the lush green landscape, hearing my friends speaking and singing in Kinyarwandan, I glanced out the window and experienced the deepest sense of the Holy Spirit running alongside the truck saying in Kinyarwandan and English simultaneously, "I'm here." Being with the people and land of Rwanda, physically reconnecting with the "main thing" of my own calling as I encountered God there, has helped me during the more frequent *bahora bahora* times.

Sustaining a commitment to your calling requires the same stuff that's required to sustain relationships. When the road gets rocky, remembering why you married the person you married, or remembering why you're worshiping at the church you are, can help to sustain your commitment. When the apostle Paul writes to the church in Corinth, he says that he considers that his present struggles are achieving something far greater: an eternal glory (see 2 Cor. 4:17).

A lot of young people, some in college and some fresh out of school, romanticize what it would be like to work for a missional coffee company. These "kids," as I call them, want to come work for us without really counting the cost. I can assure you, it is not glamorous!

Sitting and having a rare, holy conversation with Seraphine and Onesphore was only possible because of everything else that happens behind the scenes at Land of a Thousand Hills. One of those things is phone calls. We can best serve Rwandan farmers, like Seraphine and Onesphore, when we nurture relationships with the people who buy their coffee and as we develop relationships with new customers. Each of our relationship managers makes thirty to forty phone calls a day. Day in and day out, they're calling churches and prospective café owners to share our mission. And I'll unpack it further for you: 95 percent of those calls don't develop into sales! The relationship manager who's making forty calls a day, five days a week, can expect those to convert into about ten sales a week. Because I've made a lot of those calls myself, I can tell you that hearing no for nineteen out of twenty calls is not the kind of feel-good missional adventure some of our prospective employees were hoping for.

And sadly, when some realize that there is true phone-dialing, mission-sharing work to be done, they get discouraged. Many quit. Early on, we had one employee who was offended when I said that we had to focus on profit because money fueled our mission. But the *bahora bahora* work—dialing and sharing, dialing and sharing—is what allows farmers to feed themselves and their families and for customers to get a good cup of coffee.

Every phone call is *bahora bahora.*

Every email is *bahora bahora.*

Every personal meeting is *bahora bahora.*

Bahora bahora—in its vast variety of forms for different people—is what sustains a calling.

1. Pursuing your calling *bahora bahora*, little by little, means taking small steps in the right direction. What was the last small step you took to pursue your calling?

2. Who are your traveling companions? With whom do you want to grow old? Who are those people who can help you pursue your calling?

3. Right now, what is one "next step" you could take?

– 9 –

Liturgy for Life

March through Challenges

Not a lot of guys my age, pushing fifty, have a close buddy who's ninety-three years old.

But Harry Boy, as I call him, is my uncle and one of my best friends.

Harry Boy is Cockney, which means he lives within the radius of Big Ben's famous chimes. And it means he has his own language: "three" becomes "free" and a new suit is a "whistle and flute." (He employs a host of other absurd sayings, which I'm often able to understand only from context and tone.) His nose is flat, which he calls "boot nosed." And even at ninety-three, he still dresses to impress, wearing pressed shirts and chic ties.

Harry was quite the stark foil to my dad's rule-keeping. Whenever we'd visit him as children, he'd meet us at the airport with sweets. He wasn't afraid to cuss. And he would always regale us with some story of adventure. Once, while driving his Vauxhall on the narrow roads of Cornwall, he attempted to pass a man riding a horse. Skimming a bit too close, he felt a thump on the roof of his car as the rider tumbled off his horse. When he stopped to get out and check the damage, Harry Boy proceeded to curse out the horseman for denting his roof!

Not so long ago, when he was eighty-five, Harry was standing in line at the baker when he overheard a young man in his twenties being rude to the young lady working the register.

Harry commanded, "Look, mate, show the lady some respect."

The young man countered, "I'll speak as I want to," and continued with his crude rant.

Clearing his throat, Harry repeated, "Look, I said be respectful."

A second time the young man informed him, "I'll talk as I bloody well please to this tart." He then proceeded to curse the young lady and turned back to Harry, demanding, "And what are you going to do about it, old man?"

Politely but firmly, Harry informed him, "I was a boxer in World War II. I'll give you one more chance."

The young man tossed his head back and laughed for everyone in the store to hear. Then he cursed the petrified young woman yet again.

That was it. Harry pulled back his arm, winding up for a right hook, and landed a punch across the side of the man's face.

The young man, who appeared to be in shock, fell to the ground crying like a baby, moaning, "He punched me. He punched me."

When Uncle Harry recounted the story to me, he explained, "Jon, me legs are gone but me arms are still good."

Harry purchased his bread and then dutifully waited for the police to arrive. After taking his statement, one applauded him with, "Well done, old man. We need more like you."

When the paramedics arrived to help the young man, they asked Harry if he was all right. As if noticing his own body for the first time, he answered, "Yes. But my hand hurts."

When the young paramedics looked at his hand, they burst out laughing. The smart aleck's tooth had broken off in Harry's knuckles!

Harry was, as they used to say "a man's man." As a paratrooper in World War II, having no other option, he'd learned to be strong. In fact, he was one of the first soldiers to drop into Normandy on the historic D-day.

That he became a person of faith at age seventy made him no less tough.

When he was still grieving the loss of his wife, Harry had been introduced to a woman who invited him to church. Harry began attending the Church of England congregation in Romford and soon became a Christian. Today, over two decades later, he still goes to church each week. A friend from the congregation picks him up and drives him to services, and he rides the bus back to town and catches a taxi from the bus station to his home.

One Sunday the wintry weather had become so blustery that his friend wasn't able to reach him. So Harry took a taxi to the bus station and caught the bus to church. By the time church ended, the weather had gotten so severe that although the bus got him to the station, taxis stopped running. Hobbled with arthritis, Harry was stuck more than a mile from home. But get home he did.

When I asked Harry how he did it, my oldest friend answered, "Jon, look: I remembered what it was like when I was in the military service. So I said, 'Right, left! Right, left!'"

His determination came as no surprise to me.

"I knew if I kept putting one foot in front of the other," he went on to explain, "I would make it. I just marched on doing what I did so many times some seventy years ago."

He kept calm and carried on, returning to the deep rhythm his body had stored away for decades in muscle memory. That routine is what got him home safe.

We all need routines to get us home. We need routines to remember who we are. We need routines to help us live our callings.

Liturgies for Life

The particular shape of your calling will demand its own rhythm and routine. If you're in sales, putting one foot in front of the other might mean committing to making thirty calls a day. If you're a craftsman who comes home from driving a bus each day to sand wood and pound nails in the basement, you may commit to investing at least sixty minutes each day to your craft. If you're a nurse or other professional, you may decide to find one continuing education opportunity each year that enriches you and fuels you for what you were made to do.

These routines are what I call a liturgy for life.

My Anglican congregation follows a liturgy every Sunday. The liturgy, the routine we follow, means "the work of the people": *lit* meaning "together" and *ergon* meaning "work." It's the work we do together in our worship of God.

Although I'm a self-professed theology geek, trust me when I say that the order of worship really is genius. It includes confession, absolution of sin, and worship through song. We listen to the Scriptures together each week, feasting on passages from the Old Testament, Psalms, Gospels, and Epistles. We read the Book of Common Prayer together. Over time we've been formed by that shared common story. With our bodies, we physically share Christ's peace with one another and celebrate the Eucharist together.

A few things happen when a community embraces this shared liturgy.

First, within three years the community has read through the entire Bible, giving a deeper and more nuanced understanding of the Bible as a whole. Second, there is an opportunity to confess one's sin and to receive a holy assurance of forgiveness through Christ. Third, the creed functions as a counterbalance to modulate anything the preacher may have gotten wrong. (It happens.) Fourth, members have the opportunity to celebrate Christ's presence by extending a hug, handshake, or kiss with their neighbors as they offer, "Peace be with you." Finally, we create communion with each other and God as we celebrate the Eucharist.

It's a win all around, right?

As those in the recovery community like to say, "It works if you work it." Even if you've sinned, you can leave forgiven. When you don't feel God's presence, you can experience it viscerally in the bread and the wine. Or you can receive it from a friend's embrace, rather than going home hungry after a forty-five-minute sermon about what someone thinks God's Word says. You experience God's grace in community.

And liturgy always gives us the next step to take.

Mundane Soldiering

When you're seeking the courage to be you and to do good, it won't always look like awe-inspiring conversations between a Hutu and Tutsi working toward reconciliation. Often it looks much more mundane: making phone calls, poring over spread-sheets, pouring coffee. Quite often, working out your calling looks a lot like Uncle Harry soldiering on through the snow.

Right, left. Right, left. Right, left.

Half the battle—no, most of the battle—is showing up and putting one foot in front of the other.

Right, left, right, left is the rhythmic liturgy that gets you from where you are to where you're headed.

That said, our contemporary culture has lost sight of many of the liturgies for life that once provided a sustaining rhythm and meaning. In the past, more of us knew how to grieve by carving out a period to do it. Many Jewish people still "sit shiva," mourning and remembering for days after a loss. The ritual is a liturgy for grief.

When fewer young adults were heading off to college, elders in the working community who recognized a young person's talent would offer an apprenticeship through which someone could gather the skills to become proficient at a craft. The rewards of their work didn't become apparent overnight. Learning how to work the tools of the trade, working day in and day out, these learners gradually developed an instinct about their craft.

As you pursue your calling, as you seek to be you and do good, part of the liturgy that will sustain you is putting one foot in front of the other. After a while, when you've "worked" the particular liturgy that shapes your calling, you'll learn to discern the next right step.

Sometimes you'll discern that next right step because you've learned that it's time, just like Anglicans know when it's time to stand for the Gospel reading. As you pursue your calling, you'll know when it's time to get the college degree. Or quit your day job. Or keep your day job.

Other times you won't know what the next right step is, but—like Harry Boy—you'll know that you need to take a step. Right, left. Right, left.

One of the gifts of community is that those who've been through something can lead those who are learning new rhythms. When my sister was going through a divorce, she found it difficult to get out of bed. In the dead of winter, my mom laced up her winter boots, zipped up her ski jacket, put on her gloves, and pulled on her knit wool cap. After trudging down the street, she threw open the door to my sister's home and announced, "We are going for a walk! Get dressed. You are Cornish, and in Cornwall, when we get down, we walk it off."

The liturgies you establish to sustain you in your calling—completing one painting a month, journaling daily, or, if you're Cornish, walking your troubles away—are what will keep you moving when you're stuck.

Part of my own liturgy is tied to a place.

Getting Grounded at The Harp

I'd attended a large Christian conference and was unsettled by some of what I'd heard espoused there. At its conclusion, I was invited to attend a VIP dinner. But as I rubbed shoulders with many notable Christian leaders, I felt like I didn't belong. As I reflected on it, I don't think it hinged on my insecurity. I've been in similar settings many times and enjoyed them. But I noticed that all of the conversation seemed to revolve around them and their ministries. I didn't hear much that rang of courage or celebrated serving others. As a psychologist, I'm comfortable engaging people with questions about who they are. But in none of my conversations that evening did one person respond by asking about my family, my mission, or me.

Restless, I left the event early and stopped by my favorite pub, The Harp, in Roswell.

"Hello, Rev," chimed Willy the bartender when he saw me.

As I sat down he slid me a pint of Guinness, and we chatted about life and family. Willy let me know about Sloan, his four-month-old who'd recently undergone heart surgery. I shared with him a bit about how the work in Rwanda was going, and I noticed that in the presence of Willy, I found myself again.

Liturgies, like connecting with people I know and love at the pub, sustain us in good times and in more difficult ones.

Maybe you discover you are most grounded in your calling when you're able to spend time with people who share that calling. You may find refreshment at a conference among those who are like-minded and like-hearted. Or perhaps when you're marching through cold, wintry snowdrifts, you pause and dip into the home of an old friend. That friend is the one who can look you in the eye and say, "I know where you live, and you're almost there." Or perhaps when you feel overwhelmed by the pressures and demands that threaten to divert your energies from your calling, you've learned to care for yourself by blocking out downtime on your calendar or slipping away to a retreat center where you can practice silence for several days. When the cold winds blow, pay attention to those unique liturgies, rhythms, and routines that will get you home.

Right, Left. Right, Left.

When I was renovating the mill house that would become my office, the architect I'd hired fell into conflict with the Historic

Preservation Commission, and the contractor he'd hired turned out to be an alcoholic. One afternoon when I visited the project, I noticed this contractor nailing a two-by-four at an 80-degree angle, which I found disconcerting. The Commission informed me that if I wanted to continue with the project, I'd need to hire another architect. When I fired the one I had, he sued me, hiring our state representative to represent him. So I hired our town mayor! Absurdly, I was sued for "work done," which included a skylight. We didn't even have a skylight. The next step I took was to become my own general contractor. After all, I had a house to build. I pulled on my work boots, bought a pickup truck, hired subcontractors, and made it happen. Though I'd never built a house before (or an office, for that matter), I'd seen my dad run countless jobs in his pipe fitting firm. An architect friend redrew the plans. I hired an engineer named Tom, who still does projects for me today. I hired a local framer, trim carpenter, and Sheetrock crew. Each day I took the next step. I learned a lot and eventually completed the building. I had to; I didn't have the money for another contractor. I kept marching through the snow because I had to learn. Right, left. Right, left. I learned so much that I went on to build four other properties. I learned many of the liturgies that more experienced contractors already knew, but the most important one was showing up, day after day.

Living out your calling is a lot like this.

In the early years of Land of a Thousand Hills, Bukonya had almost no coffee. We'd built a $50,000 wash station and in two years had only managed to produce twenty sacks of coffee. I'd wanted specialty grade coffee, but what we'd produced wasn't up to snuff. So we hired Emmanuel Gatare, or Manny, as an agronomist who specialized in coffee growing and production.

Manny moved out of the comfortable city house he shared with his family and headed five hours away to Bukonya.

As a married man myself, I wasn't sure this was wise. But Manny insisted, "If I'm going to lead these people, I'm going to have to live with them. I need to become one of them." Manny went home only on weekends to see his family. That year he worked tirelessly on coffee quality, and his work paid off. The coffee improved. In fact, Land of a Thousand Hills placed sixth at the Cup of Excellence competition out of three hundred coffee submissions. Some of the winning coffee was auctioned off for fifty dollars a pound!

Liturgies, like living among a people to share their daily lives, are investments that sustain calling.

I've been told that Muhammad Ali, the greatest boxer of all time, hated his road work. "Road work" was the five miles a day he ran, day in and day out. And although he hated it, he persevered with the daily liturgy because it made him strong for what he enjoyed doing: fighting.

It takes maturity and discipline to embrace the more challenging parts of your calling.

A professor and friend of mine, Dave Aycock, has served four decades as a clinical psychologist. As one might imagine, much of what he's shared with his clients in the private chamber of his office has been difficult to bear. One liturgy, though, sustains him: at the end of each counseling day, Dave ceremoniously washes his hands and offers a prayer for his clients. By the end, as he shakes the water off his hands and towels them dry, he's left these individuals to God. Then he returns to his family, leaving the pains of the day to the Lord.

What we do with our bodies matters. How we choose to behave matters. When C. S. Lewis wanted to become a Christian but did not yet believe, he started by acting like a Christian. He began going to church and worshiping and behaving like Christians did. This movement of his body, resonating with the Spirit's work inside him, nurtured his belief.

Pastor and scholar Eugene Peterson has said of liturgy that the prayers we've learned tell us what to say when we don't feel like praying. Confession tells us what we should repent of even when we don't feel like it. Absolution ministers to us words of forgiveness even when we don't yet feel forgiven. And communion allows us to experience Christ, at a deep visceral level, even when we don't otherwise feel his near presence. These are the liturgies that sustain us when we need it most.

Liturgies for the Snow Storms

A few years back, a good friend of mine endured a crisis of calling in a public way. When he was at his lowest, he began receiving hate mail from others in the Christian community. During that season, "Joe" asked a friend to screen all of his emails, only passing on those that were either kind or ones that he could do something about—the ones which were in his domain. The other ones, the friend just deleted.

If Nehemiah had been online when he was serving God, these emails would have been coming from sons of Sanballat (which is also a nice phrase to interchange with profanity when you're trying not to curse!). These were the naysayers of Nehemiah's day. God had called Nehemiah to rebuild the walls of Jerusalem, and the sons of Sanballat were persistent in ridiculing him, tearing him down, and discouraging him. Though he didn't have a friend who could screen their taunts, he did pluck out their beards.

Beard plucking is what I would have liked to have done when I faced my own crisis of calling. When Land of a Thousand Hills was at its most financially vulnerable, I hired a friend to field all of the phone calls we were receiving. This "liturgy" gave me some emotional space to focus on the work that needed to be done. Another effective liturgy we put into place was hiring Tom, an interim manager, to handle the day-to-day operations of the business. And my own personal liturgies that kept me sane? I worked out when I could. I read the Scriptures. I prepared for my sermons. I maintained relationships. One management consultant advises: during the hard times, it's important to do what you do during the good times. Yet too often the natural tendency is to let the negative event create a downward spiral. It's tempting to quit marketing. To quit developing. To quit relationships. To quit, quit, quit, quit until all that's left is the mess you're in.

What have been the liturgies on your own journey that have brought you this far? Notice these and lean into them during the "snowstorm" seasons of your journey.

Then create new liturgies. Perhaps practicing a routine of morning prayer or weekly confession does not seem relevant when your life is going well. Believe me, I recognize that temptation. But when things hit the skids, these routines support and sustain you. I've experienced such palpable relief when I've blown it big-time. A favorite liturgy of mine is to pray, or even chant, the Great Litany. The Great Litany is an Anglican community prayer that leads one through confession of sin, expression of worry, and prayer for yourself, family, and the world and ends with the sacred reassurance that God has your back.

The reality is that daily liturgy doesn't look or feel glamorous. No beam of light from heaven breaks through the kitchen window to shine a halo around my head. I don't hear audible words telling me the names of new business relationships to pursue. Believe me, it's much more mundane. I usually wake up and pad downstairs in my slippers and sweats. As I brew a cup of coffee, I will pray for the farmer who grew it: his work, his family, his community. As I settle into a comfy chair in the living room and kick my slippered feet up onto a footrest, I'll read the morning prayer and review my goals. When I rise, I've been grounded by the simple liturgy.

Some liturgies prepare you to recognize your calling.

Others help you face challenges as you pursue your calling.

And some liturgies help you celebrate your calling.

As Martin Luther, the great reformer, pursued his calling, he remarked, "I have so much to do that I shall spend the first three hours in prayer." Those three hours weren't something that were wrapped up before he lived out his calling. Rather, Luther understood the way in which the routine of that liturgy sustained him throughout the day. And it wasn't a response to the overwhelming pressure Luther was under during the Reformation. It was a routine he established early in his ministry.

Warren Buffett, one of the wealthiest men on the planet, is another good example of this same kind of sustained commitment. Not only has Buffett lived in the same house for fifty-seven years, but he still walks to work, and he still applies the same system he always has to evaluate the type of project in which he'll invest. He chooses those with long-term value. Buffett explains, "Games are won by players who focus on playing the field—not by those whose eyes are glued to the scoreboard." Although it may seem counterintuitive, the best way to reach the end is to focus on the now.

Right, left. Right, left. Right, left.

Good liturgies that prepare us for our callings encourage us. From the Latin root *core*, meaning "heart," they put heart into us. Each Sunday as our community prepares to leave Saint Peter's Place, the closing prayer sends us off to live well:

> *Eternal God, heavenly Father, you have graciously accepted us as living members of your Son our Savior Jesus Christ, and you have fed us with spiritual food in the Sacrament of his Body and Blood. Send us now into the world in peace, and grant us strength and courage to love and serve you with gladness and singleness of heart, through Christ our Lord. Amen.*

This particular liturgy we use is a beautiful example as you consider the type of liturgy which will best serve you on your journey: it feeds you, strengthens you, and sends you into the world to live your calling.

For years, as I was growing up, the last words my mom would say to me as I left the house was, "Remember who you are and where you come from." But she wasn't exhorting me to remember my name or address. Much more significantly, she was reminding me to live as a Golden. To live as someone loved by her and by my dad. To live as someone whose life was meant to make a difference.

The 1993 film *Schindler's List* details the real-life efforts of businessman and factory owner Oskar Schindler. Schindler, a Nazi whose friends were military officers, employed many Jews in Krakow, due to lower costs after the German invasion. Following one neighborhood raid, Schindler was alarmed to discover that many of his employees had been murdered. In concert with one valued employee, Itzhak Stern, Schindler begins to employ Jews who would otherwise be deemed "nonessential" and deported to concentration camps.

As the film unfolds, Schindler's traumatized Jewish workers are so intent on working that they lose track of days and times. One Friday, as the sun is setting, Schindler has to remind the rabbi that it is Friday and he ought to be in preparation for the Sabbath. The vivid scene is a poignant reminder of the importance of maintaining our regular sustaining liturgies particularly in the face of crisis.

During a difficult season of our marriage, my wife and I went for a walk together, and she said what we'd both been thinking: "The relationship is pretty much dead."

Silence.

I couldn't disagree.

"So," she queried wisely, "what are we going to do about it?"

I'd just finished reading *Zen and the Art of Making a Living*, and as a result, I'd grasped the Zen concept of making things happen. During that period and since, when I've been with folks who didn't like where they were, I'd remind them, "If you don't like where you are, move. You are not a tree." Swallowing a dose of my own prescription, I decided to create movement in my marriage.

I thought what would help would be to purchase a hot tub. Each evening after work, I'd enjoy a glass of wine with my wife as we soaked in the hot tub and rekindled our relationship. Well, I never purchased the hot tub, and I don't even drink wine. But in that season we did establish a liturgy of going on walks together and of serving each other. Fifteen years later, we still do. We both still remember that stretch of our marriage as feeling like a battle. And that battle required a fresh liturgy to sustain us.

From the inception of Land of a Thousand Hills, we have always been "coffee with a story." When business was booming and when we toyed with the idea of closing shop, we continued to remember and tell the story of coffee that served customers and changed lives. In the most desperate of days, I found a way to visit Rwanda and be with my farmers. We spoke, laughed, held hands, and even got to share a *guma guma*—a beer. The practice, the liturgy, of being with them gave me the will and the energy to return to the States and deal with the challenges we were facing.

Right, left. Right, left.

Many a night, during those days, I would find solace in loading the green bean hopper, setting the controls on the roaster, and watching the coffee roast. I'd inhale the aroma of the beans. I'd listen for when it was time to drop the beans. Peaceful, I'd watch them cool. Doing what I did more frequently early on in the business grounded me and, I'm convinced, facilitated healing.

Right, left. Right, left.

During this trying season, we also focused on our team's sense of community. And though I wish that meant grabbing a beer together every night after work, our community was forged through the fire.

"Team, we may have to take a week without pay."

"Team, we may have to take a pay cut."

"Team, let's pray."

"Team, let's have fun."

Throughout, we kept telling our story and we kept selling coffee. We set up shop at conferences. We made phone calls.

When calling is in crisis, it's tempting to stop. To stop being courageous to respond to the call. But courage requires marching on.

Right, left. Right, left.

1. What is one one-foot-in-front-of-the-other routine that's gotten you through life's challenges?
2. Were any liturgies or practices mentioned that feel like they might have your name on them? Did one in particular seem as if it could be helpful to you?
3. Right now, what is the one "next step" you could take?

–10–

Destroying
the Thousandth Hill

Follow, Don't Force

Because the work commute for my day job occasionally includes jetting off to places like Rwanda, it's hard for me to wrap my mind around the depth of the roots that my grandmother had in the village where she'd been raised. In fact, before my mother was born, my grandmother had never left her village in Cornwall, England. To the day she died, she never traveled more than fifty miles from it.

The moment World War II began, Gran's husband enlisted. He'd come from a seafaring family and was eager to serve. My grandfather worked as a mine sweep on the HMS *Clyde*. During the war he swept the English Channel looking for mines.

My mom was just seven when she saw her cousin, who was working as a Western Union delivery boy, drop his rickety bike in the front yard and announce that he had a message for the woman he called "Aunt Doll." It had fallen to this fifteen-year-old to deliver the heartbreaking news that his uncle had been killed doing his dangerous job.

My mom learned too early that life includes tragedy. She also learned the value of stability and faithfulness from a devoted mother.

This steadfastness is what equipped her to follow my dad when he ventured not just beyond the village but across the seas to Canada, and then later to the United States. It sustained her through a few rocky years in her marriage while raising five children. Mom always used to say, "Whatever is to be will be." For years I saw this as a bit fatalistic and gravitated toward my dad who was the go-getter, the make-things-happen guy. I was wired more like my dad: the rugged individualist, driving hard to make things happen.

What I learned from my mother, though, is the importance of moving only when it's the right time to move. That I married a woman as steadfast and wise as my mom is likely no coincidence and most fortunate!

A few years back I'd set my mind to getting a second office building.

"Why put ourselves in debt?" Brenda asked. "Isn't one enough?"

But I saw the possibility and barreled ahead, full throttle. (Really, is there any other way?) I found a lot, built the office building, and leased it out. Though Brenda resisted, I was emboldened by my success and purchased another lot. That's when the bottom dropped out of the real estate market. And even though Brenda was more gracious and forgiving than she needed to be, I did suffer as a result of not listening to my wife's counsel.

If I had a "do over," with the magic of hindsight, I'd follow her advice and not force my own agenda.

Because I'm not completely unteachable, I learned to trust Brenda's intuition. During one season in our business, I'd been considering partnering with a businessman who'd made millions in the automotive industry and was also considering venturing into coffee. When Brenda and I had the opportunity to meet this entrepreneur and his wife for dinner, my bride and I both got a read on who this guy really was. During dinner, he spoke only of himself. He frequently cut off his wife as she was speaking. Basically, he came off as an arrogant narcissist.

When Brenda and I left the restaurant, I waited until we were back in the privacy of our car before getting the lowdown.

"So, what do you think?" I asked, starting up the engine.

Without hesitation, she replied, "No."

I don't even want to think about where I might be if I'd forced my own way in that instance. This guy did go on to form a coffee company that has bullied other companies and even employed unscrupulous means of winning accounts.

Follow, don't force.

Stepping in Sync with God's Leading

A friend of mine I'll call John has taught on some of the largest platforms around the world. And he worked hard to get there. But a few years back he told me that he was releasing some of the ambition that had landed him the large audiences and only saying yes to the invitations where he knew God was already at work.

If you can imagine, he's still staying busy!

I really like the way John sees the world. For years the style I embraced was more along the lines of: see it, say it, seize it, and then call out to God when I mess it up. But today my own prayer is to release some self-driven ambition and to work alongside God as a co-creator. Co-creatorship acknowledges that God has given me proficiencies, passions, and purpose and that there is work he would like to see done in this world. Co-creatorship involves seeing what I want to do, praying, asking what he wants to do, and then working with God to do it.

I remain curious about this line between forcing my will and following God's leading. The author of Acts writes, "Paul and his companions traveled throughout the region of Phrygia and Galatia, having been kept by the Holy Spirit from preaching the word in the province of Asia. When they came to the border of Mysia, they tried to enter Bithynia, but the Spirit of Jesus would not allow them to" (Acts 16:6–7 NIV). I've often wondered how the Spirit prevented Paul and his buddies from moving ahead.

I'm curious because for someone like me, it's hard to slow down the creative visioning and ask, "God, what do you want?" So how is it that God stops us or slows us down? I know from my own experience that sometimes God physically stops us. We're faced with an obstacle that is insurmountable. Other times we're halted as we receive and respond to an impression or inkling. I wonder if it's not similar to the way a pair of professional ballet dancers or figure skaters learn to work in concert with their partners. I also think of my mom, who's moved through life finding her places to serve and respond to God's call often within the bounds and domains allotted to her. Moving into opportunities, rather than bulldozing a path to achieve them, is a way to be responsive to God's movement.

As you embrace your calling, notice those moments when you're tempted to force your way through a door that's been closed. Perhaps you will be denied admission to the school that was at the top of your list. Maybe you'll blow the interview for what you believe to be your dream job. Or you might wake up one morning and discover that what you've been doing for the last ten years isn't what you're meant to do for the next ten. The organic nature of your calling might mean that to be faithful, you will be asked to release what may seem "good" but is not where God is leading you next. The secret to moving in sync with the One who is walking with you is to follow, not force.

Forcing Something Really Good

In 2009 I was descending into the valley of Bukonya where we'd built our first coffee washing station. For two and a half hours on a Wednesday afternoon, we'd been bumping up and down mountain roads to reach Bukonya, and as we crested the final hill I noticed some local children playing soccer. I couldn't have deduced that it was soccer because they weren't kicking anything that resembled a soccer ball I recognized. In fact, when I asked Saidi to stop the truck, I got out and saw that they were playing with a homemade ball made out of banana leaves woven together with twine. These boys and young men whom I joined in playing "football" were the sons of coffee farmers and would one day farm the land themselves. When we finished playing on the side of one of the country's thousand hills, I asked the guys if there was a soccer field nearby. I understood that the country lacked many resources, but because coffee and soccer are the two languages spoken throughout the world, it only seemed right that there should be a soccer field in this coffee-growing country.

I was super wrong.

The boys explained to me that there was not a single soccer field in all of the greater Bukonya region.

That's when I had the inkling.

What would it look like to create a soccer field for these kids?

I made a quick call to a coffee associate, Tim Schilling, who was the director of the USAID project in Rwanda. In conversation I discovered that some coffee cooperatives formed teams and hosted tournaments as a way of both helping the kids and also introducing them to coffee.

Now that I hear myself say it, it sounds like what the corner drug deal does in urban America, except that it's life-giving instead of death-dealing. Many of the children of coffee farmers had lost interest in coffee and were not aware that it could provide a viable livelihood because they'd learned that their parents made little money farming. They had no way to understand the kind of success that was possible—earning as much as four times what their parents had made!—by working with companies like Land of a Thousand Hills and others. As a result, many young people were leaving for the city when they became teenagers.

Because I knew that marrying coffee and soccer had proven to be fruitful in the Butare region, my little inkling continued to grow. In fact, when I called and mentioned it to the local bishop, he promised that when the field was done, he'd come and play!

Let me loop you in on the process that unfolds when I have an inkling.

First, I have an idea that I'm motivated to pursue.

Second, I share it, brainstorming with others and fleshing out a purpose statement.

Third, we exercise it. We share the inkling, purpose statement, and any further details with the tribe. (Tribe often means those on our staff.)

Fourth, we determine it. Specifically, we decide if we'll pursue the inkling, defer it, or decline it.

Fifth, we adventure it. One member of our tribe takes the lead, creating a strategic plan with timelines, resources, goals, team members, and benchmarks.

Sixth, when the initial inkling is realized, we celebrate it.

Seventh, we notice any new inklings that have emerged in the process.

Sounds pretty orderly, doesn't it?

But as you're no doubt discovering, when I'm captured by an inkling, I get really hopped up with both the creative process and also the thrill of power that comes from it. So when I mentioned this little inkling about a soccer field to Manny Gatare, he and I spoke to Pastor Ildephonse and were on our way! As I am prone to do, I jumped right from the inkling to the adventure.

I'd played soccer with the kids on Wednesday. I'd spoken to Tim the same day about the genius merging of soccer and coffee. Thursday morning I mentioned it to the bishop, and by Thursday afternoon Manny and I were standing outside the home of Pastor Ildephonse.

"Pastor," we ventured, "do you have a piece of land we might use?"

"Yes," he confirmed. "We have a piece of land with a small flat area next to a hill right here in the village center."

It was the best answer I could have hoped for.

"Well," I toyed, "what do you think about a soccer field?"

"That would be great!" Pastor Ildephonse confirmed. "We could get the children uniforms, and have matches and teach them. They could learn about God, soccer, and coffee."

It was a mighty triumvirate.

Pastor Ildephonse knew too well that not only had most of the youth left the coffee industry, they'd also left the church. All they knew of God and the church was that the church's previous leaders had been complicit in the genocide which has torn their country apart. As he described the loss, he looked brokenhearted.

Pastor Ildephonse sighed and said, "We have a hard time capturing them back."

Then his face lit up as he exclaimed, "Football, though! Football they naturally like."

He confirmed what was obvious among the boys I'd met. Although I couldn't figure out how, they all seemed to know about British football clubs: Manchester United, Arsenal, and Chelsea.

Pastor to pastor, I exclaimed, "So the marriage of soccer, coffee, and God really is a holy trinity! This is something I can believe in!"

One can see how, in this case, my "adventure" got ahead of my "inkling." Then I went into hyperdrive.

"Pastor," I queried, "how long do you think it would take to clear the field? Manny, where can we get soccer goals? Do you think we could get the Rwandan national soccer team involved? I'll see if I can get uniforms. Pastor, where can I get some workers? When can we start?"

Clearly, I need Brenda to be traveling with me at all times.

I left Bukonya that evening with a sense of awe and amazement, wondering if that was how God felt when deciding to create something. God needed only to think it, speak it, and create it.

And I, apparently, though not divine, was operating via the same method.

Moving Ahead at Full Throttle

My travel within Rwanda took me away from Bukonya for a week. The following Friday, with Saidi at the wheel, we rumbled back toward Bukonya. As we sailed over the last hill approaching the valley, I drank in the most glorious scene on the hillside.

Almost 150 workers, armed with hoes and shovels, were removing bags of dirt from the hill adjacent to the small flat area of land. And they were doing it with delight! I caught a glimpse of one woman who was about twenty-five years old with closely cropped hair, a red T-shirt, and a denim skirt. The smile on her face was absolutely radiant. Gripping a hoe, working stroke by stroke, she exuded the joy of work and progress. I shared her joy.

Pastor Ildephonse estimated that the work of clearing the field would take three days. Saidi and I left the project again to visit the coffee station and spend time with our team there. We returned to Kigali Friday night and then drove back to Bukonya on Saturday.

This time, though, as we crested the final hill, there seemed to be twice as many people—if that was even possible—working as before. I was shocked to see that the 120-by-80-yard patch we needed for the field had been far exceeded by the eager and industrious workers. In fact, they were in the process of taking down the entire hill! A third had already been removed, leaving a precarious cliff twelve feet high.

Anxious, I hopped out of Saidi's truck and began pacing off the length of the field, knowing we needed about 120 paces of length and 80 paces of width. As I traced both distances, I could see we'd already far exceeded the requisite excavation there. Concerned, I asked the pastor to have the workers stop.

Pastor Ildephonse used his booming outdoor preaching voice to instruct the workers to stop.

Discouraged to be stopping at 11:00 in the morning, they asked why.

"Aren't we doing a good job?" the pastor interpreted their queries for me.

"Yes, yes," I vigorously confirmed. "You're doing a good job. But we have gone *vooba vooba*. Now is the time for *bahora bahora*."

We had to stop. At the rate the project was progressing, I feared I'd be single-handedly responsible for turning Rwanda into the land of 999 hills!

Reluctantly, the workers gathered their hoes and returned home. The next day we staked out the perimeter of the field and also designated a place for spectators to stand. We made plans to terrace the land and prayed for the project. Two days later we proceeded with the order to finish the field and chalk out goals.

The field was built, but we almost lost a hill in the process.

Hear me: I'm all for inklings. I'm even all for responding to inklings by taking the next step. But the challenge for one who co-labors with the Holy Spirit is to pause to see where that next step should be. At the Bukonya soccer field, I took a step and then sprinted ahead of both God and my community.

That soccer field was a great idea. But the execution didn't unfold in the best way because I'd forced and not followed.

Responsible Following That Breeds Excellence

You may have an idea that you're certain will revolutionize the way your company does business. But if your boss doesn't think it's a world-changer, all the forcing in the world won't lead to success. You might want to do something that's an undeniable good: you want to help orphans. But you may discover that scooping impoverished children out of difficult situations isn't best for children or families. So while your calling may be to help orphans, you will walk your path most faithfully as you follow and not force. As you pursue your calling, allow God's kairos timing to unfold.

When you have an inkling, submit it to our Inkling Process (which works when it's actually applied):

1. Inkle it: What are you feeling prompted to pursue?
2. Explore it: Share the inkling with others. Brainstorm it, and flesh out a purpose statement and a few details.
3. Exercise it: Share the inkling, the purpose statement, and any details with the tribe. "Exercise" the inkling by taking it through a workout of sorts.
4. Determine it: Decide if you are going to pursue this. Is it the right kairos time? Engage it, defer it, or decline it.
5. Adventure it: Designate yourself or a member of your tribe to do it. Make it happen!
6. Celebrate it: Take time to celebrate the creation—the success—and inkle it again to see what's next!

At Land of a Thousand Hills, we always said that we did not want to be a "Christian" company. In fact, I don't believe in Christian companies. I believe that Christ came to redeem people, and as people we are called to be his children and do good work. This said, we did get our start selling coffee to churches and have continued to stay in the Christian "ghetto" subculture, so to speak. This religious subculture includes a lot of businesses and consultants that sell only to other Christians. Good folks with a product or service go to a conference and tell the churches that what they've got will help them in their ministries. So attendees buy the product and use it in their churches. It becomes a closed system that never lets the goodness of the work impact culture and community.

My friend Gabe Lyons describes how our work is to impact the world through culture. Many Christian coffee companies have little impact on culture and are, in fact, often substandard because people are willing to buy their product only because it is "Christian."

When I first started Land of a Thousand Hills, I offered a bag of beans to my seminary professor, Haddon Robinson, one of the grandfathers of modern evangelicalism. Haddon has not only served as president of Gordon-Conwell Theological Seminary, Dallas Seminary, and Denver Seminary, but he was rated one of the country's best preachers by *Christianity Today*. And he has a real heart, as I do, for the integration of faith and work.

The next day we ran into each other on campus.

"Jonathan!" he exclaimed. "I'm astonished. That is actually great coffee!"

I tried not to be offended.

"Well," I queried, "what did you expect?"

"Unfortunately," he confessed, "too often when Christians do things, they do it poorly."

He was right. I knew that people will buy "Christian" products once when they benefit a cause. But they won't buy them a second time unless they're good! My original inkling about engaging churches did grow our business. And we also put a lot of energy into Christian conferences. Then came Shawn Dunaway.

When Shawn was hired as president of Land of a Thousand Hills, he had seven years of experience under his belt working with another coffee company. Shawn would frequent our store when we were new to the game and was the first one to stop by when our roaster caught fire years ago. Even when he was working for another company, he was always helpful to us.

Though my drive had always been to pour our energies into selling coffee at more and more conferences, Shawn took one look at our books and nixed the strategy.

"Look," he said to me one day as we met to look at the finances, "they're costing us a hundred thousand dollars each year. And you yourself have said that you want to get out of the Christian ghetto."

Right and right.

"Let's put our energy elsewhere," he offered. "Let's invest some of the money we spend on conferences in internet and franchise development."

Although I heard the words he was saying and even understood the logic, something in me still resisted.

"We have all the invitations to do these conferences that most companies would give their right arm for," I protested.

But Shawn stood his ground and said we'd only do a conference if it paid for itself.

So, as a team, we canceled some of our engagements at some of the hottest conferences in the ghetto. As a result, we saved more money and made more money. But it required me slowing down, listening to Shawn, listening to my team, praying, noticing the opportunities available, and embracing a different approach.

Most entrepreneurs (these other guys, obviously not me!) are somewhat bullheaded and narcissistic. We see what's not yet there. Our drive pushes us to do things that most people won't. The rub comes when we don't know when to pause, reflect, and redirect. Today, at Land of a Thousand Hills, we're collaborating more. We interview and hire as a team. We discuss where our company should be heading.

We've learned to follow—God's direction, as well as the wisdom and leading of others—and not force.

What would it look like for you to patiently follow in lieu of forcing your own agenda? If you're launching a fledgling organization, it may mean focusing on your product, your story, and your customer and getting it right before expanding. If you're interested in teaching at a great institution, it might mean investing in a few extra years of education before applying for jobs. If you're flipping houses, not forcing may mean wading through the red tape of permits and inspections. If you crave a better job, it may mean that your wisest move is to stay a bit longer at the old one to demonstrate commitment.

Breathe deep: you have all the time you need for your calling to unfold.

1. Can you think of a time that you forced your agenda instead of following God's leading?
2. Are you naturally more impulsive, like Jonathan, or patiently thoughtful, like Brenda? How has that been expressed in your life?
3. Right now, what is one "next step" you could take?

– 11 –

When the Devil
Whispers Your Name

Stand Back Up

We were making our way to Central Baptist Church, cruising down Portage, Indiana's, County Road 700 North, when the blizzard of 1977 engulfed our 1976 wood-grain Chrysler station wagon. That my dad would not recognize an impending blizzard as a legitimate reason to skip church tells you much of what there is to know about my dad.

Thinking he could still navigate the road to church, which I didn't doubt, even my dad had trouble with the part that involved not being able to see the road. It wasn't long before we'd slid off the road into a ditch where several other cars were also stranded.

In an era without cell phones, we waited.

After about forty-five minutes, the fifteen-passenger church van that I'd finally gotten to ride in on my first summer mission trip the previous summer crept down 700 North to rescue us and the other stranded motorists. Visibility had improved enough for Mike Kellogg, my Sunday school teacher, to pick us up and take us to the safety of the church. Later, after the service, Mike dropped us all at home.

That evening, while I stayed home beside the fire, warm and cozy in my flannel pjs, my dad and my older brother Paul bundled up to face the weather emergency and set out to look for our car. When they reached the spot where we'd been rescued, bumping into a few of the men who'd ridden home in the van with us, however, our car was gone. So were the other ones that had slid off the road nearby. There was a growing sense of panic among the group until one of the men stepped on something that sounded like metal. He stomped again to listen and realized that they were all walking on top of the cars!

Wisely, I think, Dad and Paul trudged home through shifting snowdrifts, deciding to wait to rescue the car until the snow had been cleared. Monday morning, however, it was still snowing. Although they couldn't fetch the station wagon, my dad still had his sturdy work truck. And so with the same determination with which they'd set out for church the previous morning, my dad and Paul headed off toward Bethlehem Steel. This time, though, they made it as far as Highway 20, about eight miles from the house, before the state police stopped them and instructed them to turn back. Dutifully, they turned back to start driving home when the truck slid off the road. Like the wagon, it was irretrievable. There were no cars at home, so calling for help—even if they'd had a cell phone—was pointless.

They started walking. And walking. And walking.

And as the temperature began to fall, their pace did as well. The eight-mile walk home would have been a dreadful journey on foot without snow. But suddenly every single step felt monumental. Trying to step over a mound of snow that had been made by a snowplow hours earlier and now had been drifted over by another eighteen inches of snow, my dad fell on his face. Paul picked him up and they set off again. At the next intersection, they hit a slippery patch of ice and Dad fell again.

About a half mile later, Dad sat straight down in a snowbank, telling Paul he wanted to rest. They were two miles from home.

"No," countered Paul. "Come on, let's go."

Dad, who wasn't behaving like himself, argued, "No, you go ahead. It's so warm here. I just want to go to sleep. Something in me just wants to sleep."

"Dad, that's crazy," Paul insisted. "Think of the fire at home, having a warm cup of tea with Mom. Come on, Dad."

"No," Dad continued to insist, "it's so warm here. Just let me sleep awhile."

Paul knew something was wrong.

"No, stand back up, Dad!"

Paul yelled at Dad. He pleaded with him. He wanted to get help but knew he couldn't leave him. So Paul grabbed Dad's hand and pulled him up against his will to keep plowing through snowdrifts to make it home.

Paul banged on the front door and Mom came to their rescue. Easing Dad out of his hat, gloves, scarf, and jacket, they discovered he had frostbite on several fingers and toes. In fact, Mom had to pour a kettle of hot water over his boots in order to melt the ice enough to pry them off his feet!

As we pursue our courageous call, there may be seasons when we work and fight and struggle to prevail. All we can see with our eyes is winter. We can't even remember what the inevitable thaw of spring was ever like. We feel like giving up.

It's my understanding that when someone is freezing to death, the moment before he succumbs, he feels warmth all over. The nerve endings become numb, and both physically and emotionally the individual is ready and willing to be done. I think this wily voice—the foreign one Paul heard through my dad's lips—is the voice of the enemy. And when you're weary, when you're exhausted and numb, the voice begins to sound reasonable.

Standing Back Up When It Hurts

Your choice is to give up or stand up. I want to flag those moments in the journey when standing back up is much more difficult than giving up. When your GRE scores or annual job review aren't adequate, it may feel easier to give up than to stand back up. When another athlete is given your starting position, it may seem easier to give up than to stand back up. When budget cuts mean you're laid off from that job you loved, it might seem easier to give up than to stand up. When someone else gets the promotion you'd dreamed of, you might consider giving up rather than standing back up. As you face disappointments and setbacks, notice that a commitment to your calling often means choosing the more difficult path.

My childhood friend, who I'll call Mark, found out that his wife of twelve years was captured by an affair. I say captured because she was enthralled with this guy, convinced beyond reason that he was her soul mate. It was as if her heart and mind were held captive.

She'd moved out of the house and into an apartment, ready and willing to end the marriage. Mark's pastor, his mentors, his family all said, "Let her go. Take your kids and let her go."

One evening, though, when Mark's mom was staying with the kids, a friend took him out to dinner. Rather than chiming in with his own opinion, as most others had done, this guy asked Mark, "What do you want? What do you believe? What do you think God is inviting you to do?"

For Mark, the answer was a no-brainer.

"Stay with my wife," he answered.

To most everyone who knew him, Mark's answer didn't make one bit of sense. It seemed delusional. But Mark recognized that his courageous call was to stay committed to his marriage. And he did. Today, twenty-five years later, they have a strong, solid relationship.

Mark chose the more difficult way.

When I'm crushed by circumstances, wanting to give up and give in, something wells up inside me that pushes me to take a stand. For me there is nothing like a good seventies rock song to help me in the standing process. The song "Hair of the Dog" by Nazareth has come in handy many times.

Although the song inspires me, when I buckle down to pray I realize that it's not just the music that fuels me. It's God's Spirit working in concert with my spirit that strengthens me to stand.

Owning What's in Your Domain

In his book *The Courage to Be*, Paul Tillich writes that courage cannot exist in the absence of fear. Rather, courage is only demonstrated when we face our fears and overcome them. Dallas

Willard described something similar when he discussed "taking dominion" over that which is in our domain.

My oldest son, Jonny, is a talented soccer player and is relentless when he sets his mind to something. (Wonder where he gets that.) During his junior year of high school, while playing select league soccer, he went to head a ball and in the process took a shoulder to the chin, resulting in a concussion. Six weeks following recovery, he was in a tournament headed toward the goal when a defender on the other team illegally slide tackled him, resulting in a broken ankle, a lot of cussing by Jonny's teammate, and a dad who was pretty angry too. Six months later, Jonny took another concussion. During his senior year he was faced with the choice of continuing to play soccer and risk brain injury or taking a break.

Jonny ended up taking his senior year off and weathered an awful low: seeing countless chiropractors and physical therapists until finally the swelling on his brain subsided. Today he's playing soccer again and as a sophomore in college is studying physical therapy.

A few weeks ago he told me, "Dad, I went through so much for the sport I love and so many people helped me recover. For a while I was angry with God and felt like he forgot me. Now I want to help others recover from sports injuries too."

This summer he will serve as an intern by taking his healing skills to Team Rwanda, the first African cycling team to compete in the Olympics. Jonny has found a way to take dominion as he lives into his own courageous call.

The other night I was at the pub with my friend David, who was feeling defeated because the mortgage he thought he was getting for his new home had been turned down. David is a business owner, like me, and his K-1 tax form the previous year had shown a loss that had carried forward. In one respect, it was a good thing: his taxes due were far less, because although he made an excellent salary, the loss carried forward and reduced his taxable income. But while it was good for tax purposes, it didn't serve him well when applying for a mortgage.

As I listened to David, I remembered I was supposed to meet his wife at my office to strategize about how to decorate my office. I texted her to let her know I was running late. Kindly, she replied, "David needs you now more than your office needs decorating. Please stay with him."

David continued to share with me that he didn't feel too successful because he couldn't qualify for the mortgage. The blow to his identity was deeply affecting him. I could see he was struggling.

"David," I reasoned, "according to Genesis, we're to take dominion over the earth. Do you know what you're to take dominion over?"

Resigned, he shrugged and answered, "No."

"That which is in your domain," I explained. "Are the banking regulations imposed by the federal government within your domain?"

"No," he answered weakly.

"Then what can you do?" I pressed.

"I can talk to another mortgage broker?" he offered. "Yeah, I can talk to another mortgage broker." He was gathering steam now. "I can apply to a different bank. I can pray."

When David left the pub that evening, he did so with his dignity intact.

David was ready to stand back up. He just closed the loan on his new home a few days ago.

Gathering Strength to Do What We Can

The blow that had knocked him down was outside of David's domain. But sometimes we need to gather the energy and courage to stand back up when we've fallen because of our own sin. Samson, the strong man of the Bible, was like this. Enthralled by a woman with a nice set of legs, Samson relinquished his strength, his power, and to some degree his call—eventually even having his eyes gouged out and being imprisoned.

Yet even when he seemed most spiritually and physically bankrupt, Samson gathered the strength to stand. Humiliated by the evil Philistines, blinded and with his hair cut short, Samson was standing between two columns in the Philistines' idolatrous temple when he asked God for strength. With one final thrust, he pulled the columns down, sending the building tumbling down with them, thwarting more evil with his death than he had in his life (see Judg. 16).

During the blizzards of winter, however, many of us get distracted by that which is out of our domain. We become tangled up in all that we can't influence while neglecting what we can.

The Serenity Prayer written by Reinhold Niebuhr and used by so many recovery groups says it most eloquently:

> God, grant me the serenity to accept the things I cannot change,
> The courage to change the things I can,
> And the wisdom to know the difference.[9]

A priest of mine once had an insightful take on this classic verse, noting that the Cliff's Notes version of this prayer is, basically, "Flip it." It's letting go of that over which you have no influence and mustering up the strength to carry on.

One of my favorite classic movies is the 1940 film *The Mark of Zorro*, the story of a masked hero who becomes a defender of the common people. Passing the torch, the older Zorro is training the young man who will become the new Zorro. Drawing a small circle around the young man, he challenges him not to defend himself until the enemy has entered his circle. He shouldn't be concerned, taught the master, with battles outside that circle.

The young apprentice, however, engaged in fight after fight, continuing to lose. The wise sage drew the circle once more, and his young prodigy once again fled its bounds and was defeated. Finally, the master drew the circle one more time. This time the young man stayed inside, fighting only those enemies who entered the small circle. And he prevailed.

In the pursuit of your calling, and especially during the cold winters, you must draw a small circle and focus only on that which is in your control.

You may be tempted to jump to another calling, another church, another spouse. But when it is your calling, you weather the storm. Those of us who've enjoyed lives of relative comfort and privilege have too often been seduced into thinking everything should be easy. We attend seminars that teach us how anything we purpose to accomplish can be achieved in three easy steps! For $199 we're offered the foolproof "nutshell" version. My friend John, though, observes that anything that can be put in a nutshell should probably stay there. The problem, of course, is that when things get more complicated than what we'd been offered in the nutshell version, when things get hard, we bail. A psychology professor of mine taught that syrupy romantic comedies that suggest that marriage is "easy" are far more destructive to relationships than pornography.

The myth of "easy" is a seductive one.

Yet every great hero of the faith goes through a season that could be described as "winter":

Ruth: husband died; left her homeland

Esther: forced to marry; risked her life to save her people

Rahab: life of prostitution

Sarah: infertile until she was ninety

Mary, mother of Jesus: pregnant as a virgin; watched her son die a horrific death

Jesus: crucified

Paul: thorn in his flesh; imprisoned

Peter: denied Christ

Mark: bailed and left Paul

British statesman Winston Churchill knew the chill of winter. He suffered from depression. He was ridiculed by his father. He failed as a politician but faced his failures and overcame—to the point that he motivated others to the broomstick brigade in Cornwall, England. Men were so impassioned by Churchill's oratory that they marched with broomsticks because they didn't have guns!

Gandhi, one of the world's most famous leaders, who advocated nonviolence and Indian independence from Great Britain, had attempted suicide at a young age as a result of subjugation by the British Empire. Gandhi suffered from both depression and anxiety—he knew the chill of winter—but continued to lead with strength and character.

Those who are bold to embrace their callings stand back up.

Solicit the wisdom of others when you reach these pivotal deep-snow moments in your journey. My dad would not have made the best decision had my brother not been walking through the snow with him. When we're cold and wet and worn and frustrated, our judgment isn't always the most trustworthy. When you reach what appears to be an impasse in your journey, allow others to guide you home. Perhaps a colleague will see a possibility you've overlooked. Maybe a family member will push you beyond what you thought was doable. Or a friend might offer a fresh solution. Grant others you trust the privilege and freedom to guide you through your most difficult passages.

The Man Who Stands Back Up

My dad, lifelong pipe fitter, is now ninety years old. When he was about fifty-five, there was a huge pipe on a job that needed to be cleaned out. And although he was the superintendent, he was also the skinniest guy there and volunteered to clean the inside of the pipe with chlorophene to prepare it to be welded and used for high-pressure gas.

Dropping to his hands and knees, my dad scooted his way into the pipe, balancing a bucket of chlorophene. He was about halfway through the sixty-foot stretch of pipe when the fumes from the chlorophene absorbed all the oxygen in the air and my dad passed out. One of my dad's attentive men scrambled in and dragged him out to safety. Someone on the crew had called for help, and by the time he was out, the paramedics had arrived. The chlorophene had burned his lungs and reduced his lung capacity to just 50 percent of what it had been.

Specialists at Porter Memorial Hospital reported that the damage that had been done to his lungs was irreversible and that he'd continue to decline. They said he'd have to quit work and move to a climate with cleaner air, like Arizona. At fifty-five, Dad balked, thinking, "I have a church I'm involved in, a company to run, and five kids to raise." Rather than renting a moving truck, my dad started researching and discovered that lungs, even damaged ones, could be strengthened by running.

When Dad began running, each step and every breath was painful. But each time he ran, it got easier. He got up at 3:30 every morning, put on his headphones, and listened to Moody Radio as he ran. As he ran and as he prayed, he became stronger with each painful breath. Three years later, at his annual physical, his doctor reported that my dad had the lung capacity of a person with healthy lungs. Today, at ninety, he doesn't run anymore, but he still walks. His heart, lungs, blood pressure, and cholesterol are in great shape.

When a second wintry blizzard descended, my dad leaned in and stood back up.

Though a lot of us are a bit surprised when difficult seasons come our way, Jesus isn't surprised by them. He offers, "In this world you will have trouble. But take heart! I have overcome the world" (John 16:33 NIV). Jesus overcame, and he equips you to do it as well.

An Unlikely Guide

Like the lamb God provided at the altar where Abraham knelt, provision may come in uncommon packaging. It did for me in grad school, when my relationships—with my girlfriend and with my Maker—were suffering.

As the class chaplain, studying to be a psychologist and pursuing a double master's from Georgia State University and Richmont Graduate University, I was a bit embarrassed to be having relationship bumps. I'd prayed and prayed for wisdom and had received nada.

Fed up with the human relationship and the divine one, I decided to behave as if I didn't believe. I'd start making my own decisions.

During this sabbatical from belief, I'd just left my Old Testament theology course and was driving along Interstate 75 North. Far ahead I noticed a scraggly guy walking along the shoulder of the road, so I stopped to pick him up.

I introduced myself, and the young man from the road introduced himself as Jim. We hadn't gone far when Jim began reciting what sounded an awful lot like a psalm.

"Whoa," I said. "Where'd you get that?"

"As I walk the roads," Jim explained, as if it was the most obvious answer in the world, "it comes to me."

Of course it did.

"Once," Jim continued, "I was walking, like I was tonight, and a man started walking beside me, sharing all these wonderful words. Only later did I find out they were from the Bible. One moment he was with me, teaching me these words, and the next he was gone."

Jim had piqued my curiosity. I still couldn't decide whether he'd been smoking something or whether he'd really encountered the being that other people—believing people—called God.

Curious, I ventured, "So what do you think about God?"

Even in my unbelief I couldn't completely turn off the future pastor inside.

I wasn't expecting the answer Jim shared, spoken in prose as if he was telling me a story I'd never heard: "Amazing grace, how sweet the sound, that saved a wretch like me."

Jim didn't know that was my favorite hymn. In fact, during college, when I was stoned at a rock concert, the classic band Yes played it in the middle of their set. In the haze of that moment, I felt God tapping me on the shoulder, reminding me, "You can run, but I'm still with you."

Now, through Jim, I sensed that God was assuring me once again that no matter how far I might run, he was still with me.

Then Jim turned to me and instructed, "Don't ever do anything unless you really believe it. Don't do anything because people expect it of you, or because it will make you look good. Only do it if you really believe it."

Jim's words resonated within me. My sabbatical from belief was in part due to the pressures of studying Christian psychology, being the class chaplain, and expecting a perfect relationship. With Jim's encouragement, I stopped feeling like I needed to be perfect. (Though, in hindsight, I'm not sure anyone around me thought I was as perfect as I wanted to think they thought I was.)

Soon I was believing again.

When the devil calls your name, God may use the most unexpected people and opportunities to guide you if you're open to that possibility. Keep an open mind, open ears, and open hands to the surprising ways God will address you and encourage you and uplift you through others.

When the Bottom Dropped Out

Four years after Land of a Thousand Hills began, we couldn't keep up with the demand for coffee cherries our growing business required. Until 2010, I'd been financing the business through my day job as a consultant. But I knew things would need to shift when I responded to the inkling to move into working with Land of a Thousand Hills full time.

During this transitional season, I met a wealthy Christian businessman who'd done well in the manufacturing industry, and he offered to be my mentor. He helped me put together a fund in which several investors made loans of $25,000, with 10 percent interest to be paid back in twelve months. The first year was a success. And as we continued to grow, the six original investors reinvested another $150,000. The third year they did the same.

Then the bottom dropped out.

When our container of coffee from Bukonya was stolen in Mombassa, Kenya, we were forced to buy another container on the open market from an importer.

Boom.

Then another container we had on contract from our long-term partner was sold out from under us by the founder's son.

Boom.

Now not only did I not have my consulting income anymore, but we were forced to buy coffee for more than two times our budgeted amount through importers here in the US.

Boom.

We had a lease on a new warehouse and roasting facility, and we were waiting to install our new equipment. My contractor had bid $80,000 to do the job, but the landlord wanted $400,000 and insisted on doing it with his contractors. We ended up moving out on Thanksgiving weekend and were facing a lawsuit from them.

Boom.

Due to a personal crisis, our new roast master and director of production left on a dime.

Boom.

When my bank of several years failed, a construction project I was involved in ground to a sudden halt.

Boom.

Rather than pay my mortgage, I poured every dime Brenda and I had into the coffee company. I racked up my credit cards, extended my equity line, and even wagered the additional real estate we owned.

Boom.

Within a few months, the precarious house of cards started to tumble.

Against my will, one typical Wednesday night, I awoke to see the bedside clock glowing 2:30 a.m. Like so many recent nights, I realized I was most likely doomed—for one hour, two, or three—to lie awake with my thoughts. During these lonely wakeful stretches I'd worry about my company, my finances, my home, my family, and my marriage. When the worries began to crush the life out of me, I even began to wonder, "Wouldn't it be better if I wasn't here at all? What if I were to just end it?" I'd even mentally reviewed the stipulations of my life insurance policy to weigh whether or not my family would be cared for. Thankfully, God gave me the courage to soldier on.

Of course, I reached out to my Christian mentor for guidance during this trying season. I think deep inside I wanted him to fix my challenge. He was well known in the mentoring world, and I felt privileged to have him invest in me. One Saturday afternoon, as we met together sitting on a hill in front of the coffeehouse, I was reminded of a remark by Rwandan president Paul Kagame: "Nothing of significance happens in Rwanda unless it's on a hill."

Something significant did happen on the grassy hill in Roswell, Georgia, that day.

After I'd unpacked the boom-boom-boom succession of challenges and the way it was all crumbling around me, this trusted guide smoothly offered, "Why don't you trust God by turning the business over to me and the other creditors? You, of course, will have to earn your income elsewhere."

Though the words that came out of my mouth were, "I'll consider it," I now think I was in shock. Inside I was reeling with anger and hurt that this "mentor" was more concerned about getting his own investment back and building another business than helping me navigate my courageous call. I felt like the poor man in a parable Nathan told to David who'd had his only sheep stolen out from under him by a rich man (see 2 Sam. 12). While this loan was significant for my mentor, I'd poured my life, my savings, and my equity into Land of a Thousand Hills—into my calling. And now he was suggesting that I turn it all over to him.

Like the moment when David's eyes were opened and he saw things as they were, that moment on the hill was when my eyes were opened. Though this man whom I'd trusted had been a mentor, and I'm sure he meant well, he'd just suggested I exit my call.

I drove home in a daze and found Brenda out on our back porch. Numbly, I recounted the conversation. Immediately, Brenda was able to put words to my experience when she advised, "You should have said, 'I do trust God, I just don't trust you.'" After a short time feeling helplessness, the old fighter in me stood back up.

That day I grew up and made a healthy realization: I was on my own.

Standing Back Up

If Land of a Thousand Hills was going to survive and thrive, I would have to lead the way, and no one else was going to fix it. No one else could go when Abram was asked to go. I now understood that God would use me and my resources not just to fix the company but to allow it to flourish. Instead of looking toward older, wiser, wealthier men to guide what God had called me to do, I understood in a fresh way that my calling was to co-labor with God. It was my calling, and if it failed it would be because of me. For this I am thankful to my one-time mentor. That experience was probably the greatest lesson he taught me.

So I assembled a new team. I stood back up.

I took dominion over what I could by paying back debt *bahora bahora*, little by little. I released the wish that someone else would swoop in to save the company. I designated one friend to field all correspondence. Soon I hired Shawn to steer the ship and released employees who may have had good hearts but weren't allowing us to flourish. I was able to see beyond the rubble as the business began to recover.

Shawn later explained, "Jonathan, you were both wise and gracious enough to let me do my job. You are the sail on this ship pulling us along; the problem is, you didn't have a rudder. You had three accountants and none of them could tell me what the actual numbers were." He employed metrics to show that we had three salespeople who weren't doing what they needed to do. He identified those losses we'd been enduring on the Christian conference circuit. He showed that we had wonderful employee benefits but couldn't afford them, and we were overstaffed. Shawn did the job he'd been hired to do.

In that time of crisis, I stayed in my proverbial circle, fighting only the battles that were mine. I focused on what was at hand, resisting the temptation to start anything new. My inkling about starting that sheep farm? I just added it to my vision board and focused my energy on that which was in front of me.

I stood back up.

Though the devil had called my name, I didn't yield to the voice that said, "Quit life. Quit Land of a Thousand Hills. Go back to what you know, consulting." Instead, I took ownership. I partnered with the right people, hired the right person, and *bahora bahora*, we improved sales and we continued on our journey. When I was down, the way wasn't clear to me. When my dad crumpled in the snow, the way wasn't clear to him. When you face unanticipated obstacles to your calling, you may not see a way out. But as you cling to the calling once whispered in your ear, as you are willing to accept a hand extended to you, you will stand back up. This is the time when you have to use your gifts, your talents, and your passion for all they are worth. David would have faltered when facing Goliath if he continued to wear Saul's armor. He had to use his own armor, a few stones, and a slingshot. When you face your challenge, you have to use your own armor too.

About a month ago, I had the opportunity to reflect on that hard season. We hosted a company celebration to welcome new employees, say good-bye to one, and celebrate the opening of our first franchise store. I seized the rare opportunity when our whole team was gathered to thank everyone for their hard work.

Shawn's response caught me off guard when he responded, "Thank you. We are living your dream."

It was that dream, the one God had put in my heart more than ten years ago, that allowed me to stand back up.

1. Has there been a moment in your journey when standing up was more difficult than giving up? What did you do?
2. Who is the person in your life who you would trust to guide you through your most difficult passages?
3. Right now, what is one "next step" you could take?

-12-

Pitching Permanent Tents

Stay Open to New Possibilities

The sun is just setting as I look down from the mountain and notice the last bit of hurried human activity for the evening. It is late February, and I realize that the stillness down below, in the valley of Ruli, will turn into a whirlwind of activity in just a few short days.

Soon yet another coffee season will begin.

I'm at 7,356-foot elevation, atop the highest point of our coffee farm. Where I sit, we're building a small gazebo with a few hammocks for resting, enjoying, and visioning. I'd imagined that here we would build a community development center where we'd be able to host guests, provide a health clinic, and create a community gathering place, but the terrain is too steep for most guests. Climbing the narrow path at a steep near-75-degree incline is impractical for people carrying suitcases and gear for a week or days in Rwanda. Instead, the community center will be situated down the hill where it is more accessible. This higher ground where I now sit is reserved for those willing to walk the path and experience the adventure. (Or those who have no luggage.)

The new plan suits me fine. The vantage point is amazing, and I relish the moments I can spend atop the hill. Each time I climb it, I'm rewarded by a vista of our second foothold of work in Rwanda, Ruli Mountain coffee washing station. Here in Ruli the best coffee in the world is grown. Of course, I'm a bit biased! From my perch I see the work of our hands: the coffee washing station, our offices, our pulping machine, the flotation tanks, the wash channels, the fermentation tanks, the drying tables, some ten thousand coffee trees, the river, and—most importantly—the people. This year two thousand five hundred farmers and ten thousand of their family members will earn a living wage as we labor together.

God and I have navigated some precarious paths these last ten years. I've been witness to relationships being reconciled that I'd never have dreamed possible. I've seen orphans without hope go to school and begin college. I've journeyed with one young family—Sophia, Emamuel, and Yvie—who we made our family in Musanze. Brenda and I adopted these children as our own a number of years ago. They are now ready to launch into adulthood. I've seen boys like Aimee transform from being untethered wanderers to becoming men who are raising families and pursuing their own life callings. I've seen men like Rob join the journey for a season and come to know our Creator. I've witnessed the construction and implementation of the Forgiveness School, serving five hundred children of genocide survivors. I've seen our coffeehouse in Roswell burgeon from being a nearly empty venue to one in which I can often no longer find a table! I've had friends turn into enemies and have had some later return as friends again. Some Christians have helped us immensely and others have turned their backs. Muslim, Jewish, and Hindu people have all seen the value in our work and even partnered with us.

Land of a Thousand Hills is the only coffee company in the world, that I know of, that is completely vertically integrated. That means we tend the coffee from the bean to the barista, from farm to cup and every moment in between. It's an old world way of doing things, but I wouldn't have it any other way.

Five hundred billion cups of coffee are drunk every year in this world. Coffee in the US alone is a $32 billion a year industry. Specialty coffee is a small but growing portion of it. God has invited Land of a Thousand Hills into a movement where three streams come together: specialty coffee, justice, and community.

As I look out from the hilltop to see workers finishing spreading the shade net material over our newly crafted drying tables for yet another season, I wonder what's next.

I think I can anticipate what's next for the workers in Ruli, but today I'm wondering what's next for me.

Looking Forward with Open Eyes

Looking forward, I wonder what is next. Is it to be content with what's on my plate?

Is it to pore over financials so I can grow and improve the business?

Is it to settle in and rest? To coast through this next season?

I think my calling is to do more.

In fact, I'm convinced that my calling is to make space for more inklings and to wait for what is next.

In confessing that, I don't take lightly the responsibility I have to those who earn their livelihood through the work of Land of a Thousand Hills. We are a $2 million a year business. We employ twenty-five hundred farmers, six full-time staff members in Rwanda, twelve full-time staff in the US, and ten part-time staff. We supply coffee to one thousand churches, forty cafés, and three Land of a Thousand Hills coffee shops. We are just beginning our franchise model so others can join in our community and bring good coffee to their own towns and cities. Soon Land of a Thousand Hills coffee company will have local franchised coffee shops in Roanoke, Boston, Houston, Nashville, and Bradenton Beach.

If my calling was a destination, like the tip-top of this hill, I would have reached it. But it's not. It's a process, not a point. And as I watch the activity down below, the willing workers preparing the drying tables, I suspect I am being prepared for a new season as well. The challenge for me, and perhaps for you, is not to settle. It's to keep growing and building. I often say that if there wasn't work to do here, a calling that required our courage, God would take us home to heaven immediately.

Once you forge your way through the inevitable snowdrifts that threaten to thwart your calling, however your winter may look, you may be called to manage a season of steady growth. But there may also be a time to let what you've created be managed by others. The next phase of your calling might be to manage what someone else has created, taking it to the next level. That could be a classroom, a retail establishment, or a ministry.

There is a danger that what was once our passion can become our prison. I certainly recognize this in myself. Our company's "winter" was due in part to the way I continued to use my tools—risk taking, venturing, creative visioning, entrepreneurship—when what the company really needed was incremental change, control, stabilization, mentoring, and effective management.

Noticing the Itch

I once worked with a coaching client who was a multimillionaire. Seth would create a team to pursue a project, but every time a strategy and structure was put into place, he'd have a new inkling that would drive the team in a new direction! Though this worked fine for him, it was unsettling for the team and hindered the performance of the company.

Part of what Seth and I discussed was the idea that there are two types of people: hunters and farmers. Hunters scan the horizon for what might be next. They enjoy movement, quest, uncertainty. Farmers, though, like clear boundaries. They like to know that if they invest their time within certain boundaries there is a likelihood they'll be rewarded for their work. Most people's callings involve both. But if you're a farmer and find yourself spending most of your time hunting, you may choose to make a change. If you're a hunter who's forced to manage the farm, eventually you'll either destroy the farm or pursue an opportunity to move on.

One of my friends made a lot of money in his first career. Brandon is still young at forty-five, but he seems off his game. He drifts from one interest to another without ever really grabbing hold of one and digging in. Brandon seemed most alive in his first career but now has become lazy. Tired. It was as if he stopped listening and forgot who he was. He settled at some point and remains in what appears to be a permanent holding pattern.

As I gaze over the treetops, I'm aware that right now is a moment of rest, an opportunity to recover and be rejuvenated. But the itch, the inkling, is there. I wonder what God might be inviting me into.

At the beginning of the past year, I wanted to be a shepherd. Not just of people, pastoring St. Peter's Place, but an actual shepherd. I mentioned that I tacked a glossy picture of a sheep to my vision board. In my research I discovered that sheep are fruitful: they grow wool, they produce milk that is high in nutrients, and they also produce delicious meat.

Today, in the Kiryamo parish, which is two hours from where I'm standing, we're exploring what it would look like to start a farm that could be managed by Onesphere and Seraphine.

And although I'm keeping my eyes and ears open to what my future may hold, I do think that my calling is still to be a portal of grace through which others discover their life's work and the Creator of all work. In whatever form, I see that my future will hold writing, teaching, coaching, and helping others launch their own callings. And possibly some sheep shearing.

Refuse to believe the destructive myth that God will reveal a single narrow calling for your life. Our God is alive and active and delights in partnering with you for the good of his kingdom. As you mature, as you develop new competencies, as you pursue new interests, it is God's blessed whimsy to continue to call you to fresh kingdom expressions of your calling. And you can expect the unfolding of that calling to happen within the context of community.

Calling within Community

Near my home in Roswell is a development called a live-work community. In this live-work community they have built a town center, a street of restaurants, and a grocery store. It's been orchestrated to be the ideal place to live, but when I visited, I was disappointed. It seemed too contrived, too fake, too plastic, not genuine. In a word, it was too Disneyland.

I found myself wondering about the people who live there: their lives and their stories and their callings. Where was the hardware store, like the one in Roswell run by Frank and his sons Jay, Gary, and Mark? (Seriously, this store has anything you could ever hope to need.) Where was the Malaysian restaurant, Rasa Sayang, run by Daniel and his wife, Sun, who began their business in a much smaller rental space years ago? Where's the pub run by Ray and Willy where our church has gathered for thirteen years and prayed for Willy's baby daughter, Sloan, in the wake of her three heart surgeries? Where was the church where for generations people had been renewed and restored and redeemed?

Places like this new live-work community are built in a matter of months. True villages, where people and their stories and callings are woven together, take lifetimes to create. Commercial centers can be built, sometimes overnight, but true community unfolds when people live their callings and work and follow them within authentic community.

A few weeks ago, when my friend Michael came to town, I took him to The Mill Kitchen restaurant in Roswell. Our waitress had brought us menus and water, and we were perusing the menu when Ben, the head chef, came out to greet us. Ben presented with pride each of the evening's specials, making each one sound better than the last. Each of our meals was indeed exquisite. After dinner I took Michael to The Harp for a beer. Willy chatted with us for a while before returning to his work at the bar.

"This is surreal," Michael marveled. "It's like out of a movie where you actually have community and people actually know your name."

Reader, what I'd love for you to hear is that as you live your calling, you will create a true community with others who are living their calling. Lester DeKoster shares in his book *Work: The Meaning of Your Life* that work is the form in which we make ourselves useful to others. It is the greatest gift we can offer our communities. It's heartbreaking that we think of communities in which people are co-laboring, sharing goods and services and sharing their talents, as the stuff of Hollywood, while being duped into believing that quickly built commercial developments are the real thing. True villages, authentic communities, are made of people who work many years living out their callings. In fact, I don't think you can find your calling without being in community. Our communities not only help us see the needs our gifts can fulfill, they also confirm them. When former Archbishop Rowan Williams lays hands on people at confirmation—confirmation is a way of sending people out to their mission after they have come of age and owned the faith for themselves—he reminds them that they have a unique gift that God has given them for the church and the world. He reminds them that they are needed and to never forget it.

A Man Who Said Yes

I'm reminded once again of Abraham, chilling in front of his tent, looking up at the stars. I think that he could have been feeling a restlessness in his spirit to be doing something different. By all accounts, he'd made it. Although he didn't have children, he had Sarah, and he had wealth, land, sheep, cattle. But I imagine there was a restlessness that night that drove him out in front of his tent—no doubt sipping a good cup of coffee—when he sensed the voice of the One who was, the One who is, and the One who will be whisper, "Get up and go."

"Where?"

"To a place I will show you."

It's funny that we've lifted up Abraham as an iconic figure with a "first-rate" calling from God. In reality, every one of us finds our calling as we go. Abraham was no different.

So Abraham went.

He went and stayed for a while until the Lord said "go" again.

And then Abraham went.

Again.

Abraham wasn't perfect. He slept with his wife's servant, Hagar, to produce an heir. He jumped to plan B instead of trusting God that plan A would unfold in God's time. And even when he received the child God had promised, he still lived in a tent.

A lot of us who put down payments on places in the next commercial development much prefer mansions to tents. We'd rather be settled than be sojourners.

When we're honest, a lot of us would rather settle.

If I had to get up and go tomorrow, I'd need to sell my house, my office building, and my car. But if I lived in a tent—though I don't mean to glamorize such living—I'd be better prepared to move.

Abraham could have bought a lot and built a stone foundation, but he didn't. When the time came, he had to buy a small plot of land even to be able to bury his wife.

Why didn't Abraham settle?

My hunch is that it's because he understood that his call was to be ready to move when God invited him.

The author of Hebrews echoes God's call to this father of the faith:

> By faith Abraham obeyed when he was called to set out for a place that he was to receive as an inheritance; and he set out, not knowing where he was going. By faith he stayed for a time in the land he had been promised, as in a foreign land, living in tents, as did Isaac and Jacob, who were heirs with him of the same promise. For he looked forward to the city that has foundations, whose architect and builder is God. (Hebrews 11:8–10 NRSV)

Though Abraham and Sarah lived out their calling in the land to which they'd been sent, they understood that their permanent home was with God in a city of which he would be the architect.

Speak, Lord; Your Servant Is Listening

An integral part of our callings is to be ready to move. Perhaps you'll be called to a physical move or a new position within your organization. Maybe your sense of call will lead you into a fruitful new expression of the work you've been called to do. To partner with God for kingdom purposes is to be ready to move as God leads. You can be assured that in this process you will need to be you to do good.

Oswald Chambers said that the greatest deterrent to hearing God's call for today is yesterday's call. And while I don't think God is switching up our callings day by day, the God who lives does long to co-create with you. God didn't create a permanent kingdom for Abraham, and he doesn't for you either. As we manage the domain that we've been given, we also listen for God's gentle, and sometimes not so gentle, leading.

Yesterday I reviewed the lectionary readings for this coming Sunday. I tell you, these texts were hand-delivered from the Almighty himself: from God's mouth, through my words, to your heart, I pray.

The Old Testament reading from 1 Samuel 3:1–20 was the story of Samuel serving in the temple under Eli. God hadn't been doing a lot of talking to Eli's generation, but he addressed Samuel—by name nonetheless—when Samuel lay down to sleep. And although it took a few tries for Samuel to understand, he got the message.

> Then the LORD called, "Samuel! Samuel!" and he said, "Here I am!" and ran to Eli, and said, "Here I am, for you called me." But he said, "I did not call; lie down again." So he went and lay down. The LORD called again, "Samuel!" Samuel got up and went to Eli, and said, "Here I am, for you called me." But he said, "I did not call, my son; lie down again." Now Samuel did not yet know the LORD, and the word of the LORD had not yet been revealed to him. The LORD called Samuel again, a third time. And he got up and went to Eli, and said, "Here I am, for you called me." Then Eli perceived that the LORD was calling the boy. Therefore Eli said to Samuel, "Go, lie down; and if he calls you, you shall say, 'Speak, LORD, for your servant is listening.'" So Samuel went and lay down in his place.
>
> Now the LORD came and stood there, calling as before, "Samuel! Samuel!" And Samuel said, "Speak, for your servant is listening." (1 Samuel 3:4–10 NRSV)

Samuel knew he was hearing something, but he wasn't sure what it was.

Intimately Known

The second lectionary reading that same day was from Psalm 139.

> O Lord, you have searched me and known me.
> You know when I sit down and when I rise up;
>> you discern my thoughts from far away.
> You search out my path and my lying down,
>> and are acquainted with all my ways.
> Even before a word is on my tongue,
>> O Lord, you know it completely. . . .
>
> For it was you who formed my inward parts;
>> you knit me together in my mother's womb.
> I praise you, for I am fearfully and wonderfully made.
>> Wonderful are your works;
> that I know very well.
>> My frame was not hidden from you,
> when I was being made in secret,
>> intricately woven in the depths of the earth.
> Your eyes beheld my unformed substance.
> In your book were written
>> all the days that were formed for me,
>> when none of them as yet existed.
>
> Psalm 139:1–4, 13–16 NRSV

Through this psalm I'm reassured that just as God knew David intimately, God also knows me. He knew me when I was knit together in my mother's womb. He knows when I sit down behind my desk in my spinning office chair, and he knows when I get up to fetch another cup of coffee. He knows when I'm wily and stubborn and sinful. God knows each of the days that were ordained for my life—the one when I married

Brenda, the one when we welcomed our first son into the world, and all the days that are yet to come. I am comforted by being known.

Set Free to Follow

The same day's epistle reading, 1 Corinthians 6:11–20, was carved from Paul's letter to the church in Corinth. It reminds me that just as food was made for the belly, so I have been made for the Lord, bought at a price to belong to God. We've not been made for lesser things. We've been made for mighty, bold, courageous things. Today you and I may not find ourselves bound to a prostitute as Paul says, but we may be enslaved to a mammoth mortgage. Or our jobs. Or an addiction. Paul reminds us that we are made for the Lord, to be one with him.

Your calling is more than your role, more than your job, more than the way you earn your living. It is that for which you're made.

Lastly, in the Gospel reading, Jesus calls Philip to follow him as he is going about his mission.

> The next day Jesus decided to go to Galilee. He found Philip and said to him, "Follow me." (John 1:43 NRSV)

Jesus's calling wasn't done in isolation, and neither is ours. And when Jesus calls Philip, Philip calls Nathaniel.

Nathaniel has just had some meditation time under the fig tree. I imagine he might have been wrestling with the state of Judaism, or possibly where he was heading in his own life. This is what Jewish guys did underneath fig trees: they thought through life under the shade of a tree on a hot day.

What happened next was sort of the ancient equivalent of copying the wrong person on an email or hitting Reply All when you really only meant to gripe to one person about the other. When Philip told his friend that they'd found the one of whom Moses wrote, Nathaniel blurted out, "Can anything good come out of Nazareth?" (John 1:46 NRSV). And what Nathaniel experiences, in this odd exchange—when he's sort of busted by the guy he was grumping about—is being known by Jesus. When Jesus spoke to Nathaniel, he said, "Here is truly an Israelite in whom there is no deceit!" (John 1:47 NRSV). Jesus accepted Nathaniel *and* his questioning.

In drawing Nathaniel into Jesus's own calling as the Son of God, Jesus also welcomed Nathaniel to discover his own calling.

When God Is Up To a New Thing

When I married Brenda, she was a career woman and wasn't sure if she wanted to have children. One year after we married, though, she gave birth to Jonny, and she continued to work: two days she worked from home while caring for Jonny, two days I did, and one day we had a nanny. The sweetness of those days surprised me, and I realized then that part of my call was to raise my son as a stay-at-home dad. Brenda had a similar experience. So when her boss gave her an ultimatum—be here full time or not at all—the choice wasn't a difficult one for Brenda. Although she'd poured her life into helping at-risk women, she sensed clearly that her calling in the next phase of life, however long that might be, was to invest in our family. At the time, Brenda was making $40,000 a year and all of our insurance was through her job. I'd just started my consulting business, was working out of our screened-in porch, and had billed a whopping $10,000 the previous year. When we discussed how we could make it financially, it was clear that the desire of her heart was to stay home. I wanted that for her too. That was the beginning of her twenty-year work of love investment in our sons. We tightened our belts, I worked long and hard, and we never went hungry.

Today, twenty years later, Brenda is being trained as a spiritual director. With all but one of our sons grown, she noticed the inkling to use her gift of helping in a new way. Though she has two master's degrees in counseling and is a certified addiction specialist, this next phase of her journey involves helping people in the context of spiritual direction. Brenda explains it this way: it's about helping others discover how God is already at work in their lives.

Brenda stayed open to the new thing God wanted to do in her and through her.

God's been up to something new in my friend Greg's life as well. Like me, Greg is a bit of a serial entrepreneur. He started as a golf pro, then launched a furniture business, and after several successful years he decided it was time to sell. In his next venture, he purchased a sign company. Because the previous owner had fudged the books, Greg had his hands full turning the business around. With wisdom and hard work, he made the business a success.

As the sign business began to thrive, the next inkling took root in Greg's heart and mind. He wondered, "What if I could use my business skills to help others in a new way?" So, while continuing to run the business, Greg went back to school to get his teaching certificate. Because I've had the privilege of speaking at a few of Greg's business classes at our local high school, I can assure you that my friend is pursuing his calling by using his talent in a fresh, bold way.

Land of a Thousand Hills was in its fifth year, during the difficult season that threatened the viability of the business, when I sat with my friend and client, Bob.

"I'm thinking about going back to coaching and consulting," I told him, as if I was in a men's store trying it on for size. The thought had been rattling in my mind for a while.

Bob gasped. "Did you hear what you just said?"

"Yes," I answered, hesitantly, not sure what he was driving at. "I said I'm thinking about going back to coaching and consulting."

Wisely, I think, Bob challenged me, "Never go back to something. Go forward."

So I did.

I leaned into Land of a Thousand Hills, marched through that devilish season of challenges, and stood back up.

Today the business is thriving and growing. And in this new moment, I have an inkling to use my coaching and consulting gift to help others find their call. Now that I've had the experience and adventure of having pursued Land of a Thousand Hills, I feel even better equipped to help others find and grab hold of their courageous call.

This time, it's not going backward. It's moving forward.

As you look toward the hills, what do you see in your future? Perhaps the road you've been on continues as far as the eye can see. Or perhaps there's a bend or a dip that's hiding what's ahead. I am confident that whether the landscape of your call is entirely evident or whether you're still discovering it, God will continue to lead you into the calling for which you were made.

Me too.

Standing on top of the tallest hill in the village, I catch the last glimpses of Ruli Mountain coffee washing station before the sun sets. In the distance, I see Manny running up the road to get me. Tonight we'll travel down the mountain, and tomorrow we'll rumble up to Kiryamo to check on our sheep and visit with our shepherds Onesphore and Seraphine as they live out their calling.

As you take the next step on your journey, my prayer is that you will *be you* and *do good*.

1. Are you wired more like a hunter or a farmer? How has that expressed itself in your sense of call?
2. Do you have a sense of what God has next for you? Any inklings?
3. Right now, what is the one "next step" you could take?

Acknowledgments

I am especially grateful for those courageous souls who have co-labored with me in my calling.

To all to the resilient, loving, and life-embracing farmers of Rwanda: I have received more from you than I will ever be able to give. The way you have learned to forgive and flourish amazes me.

Next, thanks to my team at Land of a Thousand Hills Coffee Company, some of whom are still with me while others have moved on to be themselves and do good elsewhere.

Then to the generation that followed their call before me: Dad and Mom, who through their adventure of living and being married some sixty-six years have taught me so much about faithfulness, and Uncle Harry, who taught me to be tough and have fun.

Anyone who learns to be who God created them to be and engage in good has to do so within community. For me, this has been St. Peter's Place, a small, strong Anglican community that works out our faith together through common prayer, the breaking of bread, and love. Thank you for trekking through life with me.

Finally, to my wonderful co-explorer in life, Brenda: it would be very hard to be me and do good without you. Your wise, gentle crafting of a home and life allow me to venture out. Our sons are living results of the greatness that results from being you and doing good together!

Notes

1. See "Garages," television ad for Cadillac CTS Sedan, aired September 5, 2014, available online at http://www.ispot.tv/ad/76nQ/2014-cadillac-cts-sedan-garages. Accessed July 8, 2015.

2. Brené Brown, *The Gifts of Imperfection* (Center City, MN: Hazelden, 2010), 6.

3. The 7 Principles of Lifeswork program clarifies purpose, passion, people, provision, and proficiency.

4. This is horrible advice.

5. Bob Goff, *Love Does* (Nashville: Thomas Nelson, 2012), xiv.

6. Jean Vanier, *Becoming Human* (Mahwah, NJ: Paulist Press, 1998), 28.

7. Friedrich Nietzsche, *Beyond Good and Evil*, trans. Helen Zimmern (London: 1907), sec. 188.

8. See Lauren Winner, *Girl Meets God* (Chapel Hill, NC: Algonquin, 2002).

9. For more on the background and versions of this prayer, see "Serenity Prayer," Wikipedia, modified June 15, 2015, https://en.wikipedia.org/wiki/Serenity_Prayer. Accessed July 13, 2015.

Jonathan David Golden is the founder of Land of a Thousand Hills, a multimillion dollar coffee company that provides a living wage to more than 2,500 farmers in Rwanda. He and his company have been featured by CNN, Fox News, *Christianity Today*, *Relevant*, *The Atlanta Journal-Constitution*, and *Charisma*. Jonathan has spoken and been featured at Catalyst, Q, Story, Exponential, Velocity, Ignite, Collyde, and Orange conferences and has toured with Third Day, TobyMac, and Switchfoot. He is also an ordained Anglican priest at St. Peter's Place in Roswell, Georgia. Join the story at www.BeYouDoGood.com.

LIKE THIS
BOOK?
Consider sharing it with others!

- Share or mention the book on your social media platforms. Use the hashtag **#beyoudogood**.

- Write a book review on your blog or on a retailer site.

- Pick up a copy for friends, family, or strangers! Anyone who you think would enjoy and be challenged by its message.

- Share this message on Twitter or Facebook: **"I loved #beyoudogood by @jonathandgolden // beyoudogood.com @ReadBakerBooks"**

- Recommend this book for your church, workplace, book club, or class.

- Follow Baker Books on social media and tell us what you like.

 Facebook.com/ReadBakerBooks

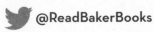 @ReadBakerBooks